HOW TO CHANGE TOXIC RELATIONSHIPS

HOW TO CHANGE TOXIC RELATIONSHIPS

SAVANNAH SMOKE, MSH, RMT

This book is a work of non-fiction. Names have been changed to protect the idenify of the the people used in the examples. Any resemblance to actual persons, living or dead, events, or locales is entirely coincidental.

Personal medical disclaimer:

All of the following is presented as personal opinion and does not mean to be medical advice nor in anyway to be an endorsement of any of the treatments or items listed herein. Always consult a physician for all medical advice. This document can contain errors and omissions and should not take the place of licensed medical care. I am a spiritualist not a medical doctor. These are my experiences with health and the keys to immunity are my personal opinion.

For information contact; address www.narcissistnirvana.com or you can contact the author at healingbysmoke@gmail.com.

Book and Cover design by Designer

ISBN: 123456789

First Edition: March 2020

Print ISBN number 978-1-948881-00-5

eBook ISBN number 978-1-94881-01-2

10 9 8 7 6 5 4 3 2 1

Table of Contents

Introduction

SHOULDN'T SOMEONE GIVE us a road map to personality disorders when we are born? Of all the things we learn some of the most crucial, beneficial information is completely missed! We are here haphazardly building ourselves through this journey called life. As we grow into adults, we find ourselves locked into toxic situations and relationships that become painful aspects of our lives. They do not educate us on how to handle these challenging and hurtful people or encounters.

Right now, we are in a fascinating time of soul healing and enlightenment!

All along difficult "toxic" personalities have been designed to teach us our inner wounds and unhealed parts. Yet I never knew. No one let me in on the secret. Once I got educated, I started to understand exactly what was going on. Spiritually, mentally, emotionally, and physically, I began to sharpen my wits. I started training, healing, and growing through dun, dun, dun… The Narcissists on Battlefield Earth.

I am eternally grateful. You will be too. Through the course of this book, I will unravel the science and spiritual purpose of these relationships. You will know how to catapult over ALL their nonsense with ease and grace. No one has taught us these principles. We have been operating blind with these personalities, and now it's time to turn the tables.

Take control and beat the narcissists, toxic, controlling, and manipulative personalities at their own game. Not by joining them in their tactics but healing, growing, and evolving into the person you are destined to become. If you are a target to their techniques, there are elements of you that attracted the relationship. You just need to open your eyes in new ways and do the inner soul work to stop stepping in their trap.

Oh, the beauty when you see your experiences with them in a new light. The blinders you've been looking through fall off. All the systems of suffering they set up for you become blazingly obvious. Not only that, but you understand their purpose. You are no longer confused by their crazy-making behaviors. As you read and apply the knowledge in these pages you will learn the specific tools, techniques, and elements to break through the barriers.

You will have a new inner strength and sense of power, knowing you can deal with these personalities effortlessly. You are no longer their pinball being looped into their nonsense, emotionally crushed, mentally brainwashed, or physically drained. The days of being a victim because they appealed to your compassionate heart are over. All your weaknesses, naïve perspective, and gullible ways you have turned around.

The mystery of why these personalities keep coming into your life is completely unraveled. You realize if you are a victim to narcissists, you attracted them by being a match. This is where we level up and get accountable. Our souls line up and these invisible magnetic charges bind us together. You have the exact opposite charge or unhealthy and out of balance opposing quality. Only by healing that inner wound and balancing our dysfunctions can we stop playing our role in the relationship.

Both parties become a mirror to inner imbalances:

Naïve/Gullible attracts Liar/Manipulator

Non-Confrontational attracts Confrontational

Insecure/Self-Doubt attracts Over Confident/Ego Maniac

Overly Sensitive attracts Insensitive

Cannot Receive attracts Cannot Give

No Personal Boundaries attracts Over Steps Your Boundaries

Accepts All Blame attracts Can't Be Responsible for Blame

This book will teach you exactly how to stand rock-solid, completely peel away all narcissistic supply, and balance your internal scales. Imagine how you will feel when confronting the narcissist as a healthy, whole, an educated version of YOU! All the tactics, techniques, and tools they used and why you fell for them become obvious. You no longer fit in as their victim.

We will dive deep into these techniques. You will see how to unravel your own weaknesses and unhealed traumas. Your soul wounds created the need for them in your life. The personality characteristics work together like gears on a clock. Suffering ticking away, time is moving yet standing still. Now you have all the answers to transform, heal, and evolve.

For example,

Gaslighting: The universe has a consequence for those not fully present in the moment. Now you have decided to start paying attention and taking notes. You don't let the twisted illusion of the narcissist disillusion you. They used to win at this head game because they would lie and manipulate situations, people, and events to convince you they are right. Before you questioned and doubted yourself, but now you are interviewing and challenging them. You know their twisted reality and don't fall into their trap. Those situations that used to leave you confused and frazzled become opportunities to have your opinion be voiced. The daydreaming, non-confrontational, insecure, and overly sensitive part of you is no longer running your show.

Spiritual growth: Believing, trusting, and standing up for your gut feeling and intuition. Becoming present in reality rather than daydreaming and floating through life. Self-trust rather than self-skepticism.

If you want a deeper look into this concept you can find my YouTube Video explanation by clicking this link. https://www.youtube.com/watch?v=68DL1smdbnE&t=4s

Smear Campaigns: The grand actor is up to their tricks and is using others against you. They have portrayed themselves as the innocent victim. You are the abuser, toxic person, and dysfunctional part of the relationship. This can be so challenging when you know lies have been twisted against you. Before this would have frustrated you to no end. Now you realize you have to know who you are, what you stand for, and your principles to gain inner strength. No matter what anyone else thinks or who falls prey to their charms and manipulations, you know who you are and the truth. You are using the experience to gain inner solidity and be un-wavered by other's opinions.

> *Spiritual growth: Insecure to the views and criticisms of others becomes secure and confident despite how others see you. There is no other way to develop this without these personality types smearing your name, twisting lies against you, and manipulating situations to make others have false opinions.*

These are just a few brief examples where we take all the information we have learned and apply our new healed authentic self into our life. That's the ticket to reflecting a new reality. All the tactics and techniques we previously saw as toxic facilitate our growth. We are so grateful to them for their placement on our path.

Coming from a background of attracting "toxic" people has taught me so many things. The biggest realization has been the fact they were mirroring where I was toxic to myself. None of it was actually about them. Working on myself, I've become stronger than I imagined. I have fought wars with these crazy-making personalities and remained calm. I can call out every tactic in my mind that's being used against me and how to combat them. Not later, but at the moment. No one manipulates me or my emotions anymore. I am finally in love with my life and who I am rather than spending countless hours running victim stories in my head or trying to make sense of their behaviors.

You can do it too.

In this book, I'm handing you the keys. You must put them in the ignition and drive. My struggles, pain, and dysfunctional, unhealthy cycles have become the force of passion to help others heal, evolve, and move out of these toxic relationships. Trust me. They are not going anywhere, just continuing to create your suffering until you learn what they are designed to teach you.

You might have already noticed this… have you ever seen someone leave one toxic relationship to sign up with another carbon copy personality? Or you realize that you are in a toxic relationship, but cannot figure out why you can't let them go?!?! Am I addicted to this dysfunctional mess?!?! It's so frazzling seeing these repeat patterns and toxic attractions but not knowing how to get out. These personality types and situations keep coming back to us over and over for specific reasons.

We are broken and must finally heal and evolve beyond them. Knowing exactly how, why, and what about us needs to take action, heal, develop, and do the inner work is crucial. If we turn a blind eye, or walk away without working on us, the pattern continues.

Once you do the inner work, exciting things happen. You interact with them unaffected by their tactics or manipulations. You no longer need to hide from the world or difficult personalities. You can be in any life situation or relationship and be the healthy version of yourself, unaffected by external forces.

The world around you is a mirror and the laws of attraction bind us all together. You can't attract someone who unconditionally loves you until you unconditionally love yourself. If you can't make yourself a priority, you won't attract people who do. If you haven't learned to support yourself, you can't attract those who support you. This list could go on and on. In fact, maybe you should make one. Use how people treat you as a guide to see the hidden inner world you have with yourself.

If there is suffering in the outside world, it's coming from an inner imbalance. Using the toxic people in the outside to balance our internal scales, dysfunctions, and heal our inner wounds is a priceless gift. We have to get clear on all the elements. What are their personality traits? What are mine? How do they work together? What is happening mentally, emotionally, energetically, and spiritually in our interactions with one another?

Absolutely the best investment you can make is in yourself. Learning, studying, and using the relationships to get stronger, heal our wounded parts, and step over the spiritual hurdles in life completely changes everything. Take the journey with me and learn all the techniques, principles, tools, and self-healing elements needed to ignite that inner God/Goddess warrior that has been waiting to wake up inside you.

The information you are about to unveil you won't find in any other books on the market. That's why I committed myself to write what you're about to read. There are so many people suffering with no idea of how, why, or what to learn from it. They find they leave one partner taking the prescribed "no contact" advice to re-create the next narcissistic relationship with the same issues, just a new person. Or they remain locked into the partnership unable to leave, but need to learn how to handle the toxic person for their own sanity. Why are they like this and what do I do? Within these pages are the missing keys.

The more people who can assimilate, use these tools, pass them along, and truly heal, the faster we can move into the Age of Enlightenment!

CHAPTER 1
WELCOME TO THE JUNGLE

WHEN THE TERM "narcissist" and "toxic people" crossed my path, the lightbulb definitely turned on. My jaw dropped over and over as I began to research. Connecting the dots to manipulative and controlling people in my life floored me. Gah! I've been so naïve and gullible. All this new and pertinent information would have been useful to know, like at birth. Not two marriages and three children deep into the deal. Why hadn't it occurred to me? There are people who I thought were my friends that are intentionally hurting me and others for their own advantage.

Maybe you felt that same way too. This thought of people operating as narcissists with all their techniques and tactics is like learning a foreign language. I'm not talking about the obvious evil people that are raping, stealing, and murdering. They are easy to spot. We wouldn't get tangled up with them. This layer of personality appears to be genuinely interested in you, kind, and helpful. The deceptions aren't easy to see. They are skilled at the tango of looking to be a fantastic person while they use, abuse, and sabotage everything.

Even in researching the topic and connecting all the dots, I just didn't want to believe it. My whole life, I had made excuses for why seemingly good people had moments of being bad people. I would blame it on several things. Childhood trauma, they had a bad day, or someone hurt them. Who wouldn't have issues from this screwed up world we live in? You know the saying, "Hurt people hurt people." If we could fix, heal, and save everyone this messy nightmare would end.

I realized that I was living in a fairytale illusion, refusing to see the truth, exactly what the experts said about the narcissist.

I was such a huge advocate of making the best of everyone and turning the other cheek. Yet, that just led me to being a doormat allowing others to walk all over me while I made excuses for them. Isn't that what we've been told we should do here as a "good person"? Forgive others for their imperfections and hope they do the same for us.

Unconditional love.

Some horrific things are going on. How can I justify them? How can I not get wound up and passionate about so many offenses happening in this world? Not just with the narcissists in my life but on a huge global level. Honestly, before all of this inner awakening happened, I never realized there was a purpose to this madness.

I just felt lost here.

If there is a God, what is he doing, letting people run around destroying everything?

What's the real reason I'm alive?

I was coasting along in life surviving but in a miserable, painful place.

Waiting for the deadline… death, which seemed like the only escape.

I could see no way out of suffering. I was spinning my wheels one day leading into the next. At the core of my soul, I felt desperately alone, miserable, and shattered. That's precisely where I was when things started to unravel. So many epiphany moments happened. This began the wheels of change and a grand awakening in my life. Everything fell into place to open my eyes.

I realized I am NOT a spirit walking through Earth, trying to make it through enough tomorrows to see if I get access into the pearly, white gates of heaven. I am a spiritual being full of these energetic connections, wounded parts, dysfunctional patterns, spiritual imbalances, and karmic ties. It was a massive revelation to me that time was standing still in some ways. My repeat patterns became obvious. You will see yours too, or maybe you already have. You just don't know what to do about them. After reading all the books, blogs, and resources on toxic people, you've seen no real results.

You are more educated. That's an important step. You have a new fancy vocabulary for their techniques. Gaslighting, triangulating, lovebombing, discard, devalue, smear campaigns and a whole list of explanations for narcissistic behavior patterns. This is helpful to know but it doesn't get you out of the wheel of suffering. You are still locked into the crazy-makers.

Maybe you missed the same big memo I did when you were growing up. You are in a physical body attracting certain people and situations just like a MAGNET to teach you the spaces you have yet to HEAL. This idea, what we put out in the world comes back to us is simply not true. Be nice to others, they will be nice to you. Help people and when you need help the favor will return. Well then, when is that going to show up? I just keep attracting toxic people and narcissists.

Newsflash, it's never going to show up. Karma is not what we have been led to believe. Just like most of the information we receive. If you realize this already you may be interested in my **YouTube Channel, "Truth Bomber TV"** or click this link https://www.youtube.com/channel/UCUmMXxIgUPvmYT0mlLs3ilA?. You are in battlefield Earth, the ultimate jungle. Have you watched that movie made by Disney, "The Jungle Book"? Here's Mowgli meeting these characters, the smooth-talking ape, slithery python, fearsome tiger, free-spirited bear, and he has to navigate. In that journey, he learns all kinds of life lessons. If every single experience had not happened exactly how it did, he could have never grown and evolved.

That required a lot of different personalities to provide those experiences. Why not learn what this jungle, we call Earth, can teach you? You can do the inner work to heal and transcend. In fact, it's the only way out of the wheel of suffering. You have to re-educate yourself on a lot of new concepts. This solves a lot of unanswered questions plus gives you the keys to take back your life.

Maybe you're in a tight corner trapped with this personality? Perhaps you have children with a narcissist, controlling, or manipulative spouse and you don't want to tear your family apart? Maybe you're in a great position at your company but have specific people you don't know how to deal with? What if your child is a narcissist? You cannot leave them. We don't intentionally end up in abusive relationships. That's for sure!

These triangles where we can't escape are necessary. We corner ourselves in these relationships on purpose. If we could easily disconnect from them and walk away, we wouldn't learn what they are designed to teach us. That's how we get entangled as our energies lock us into one another. As much as we may want to hate them, they have a divine spiritual purpose in our lives. I know it seems like such a stretch to think someone so capable of deeply inflicting pain has an actual role to play in your development, but it is the truth.

If you do not deal with the shattered parts of you that attracted this relationship, guess what happens when you go "no contact". The next narcissist steps up to the plate to work out whatever is unresolved inside of you. That's why most people leave one abusive relationship to sign up with the next person, who is almost exactly like the ex that they left. I know this is true. I have done it and watched others do it too. Or maybe they lacked compassion for someone who was in a narcissistic triangle. They made judgments that created karma. We will get to the heart of karma and it's true meaning soon.

I should clarify if you are dealing with a physically abusive person, you need to leave. You can't stand up for yourself when it will lead to bruises and broken bones. If you don't have secure connections with supportive people, there are so many safe houses you can contact. I do still recommend reading the book. You still need healing from emotional, mental, and spiritual abuse, which is the focus.

Speaking from experience, I can tell you that if you make a stand and leave someone physically abusive you set the standard within your own being. I am worthy of a relationship and will make clear cut decisions to walk away from partners that physically hurt me. Whatever other issues you have not resolved will come up in a new partner. They will not physically hurt you but emotional abuse is just as damaging. The wounds just don't show up on the outside body like physical abuse does.

Making a stand to honor and love yourself enough to not be physically abused is critical to our health and well-being. Lots of people who are in these types of relationships often do not understand why they stay, but they do. This book will clarify and answer those questions for you. Let's face it sometimes we do things we know don't make sense. Other people can't understand why we just don't leave and that can be even more isolating. Exactly what we don't need.

My first husband was physically abusive. I did leave. I did go back. I left again, and the cycle went on. I wanted to believe him. I wanted to have things be the fairytale. I didn't understand how I could love him, but I really thought I did. If you are in that same position wanting to leave but you stay, I understand. I love and support you. I am lucky I had a great family, a safe haven. Even in that I broke away to just go back to him many times. The final split up was gut-wrenching and heartbreaking. If I had understood these concepts and truly healed, I would have saved myself covert narcissist husband number two.

What I found interesting in my research is emotional and physical abuse run the same response pattern in our brain. If you are dealing with a covert narcissist, no one knows what is going on behind closed doors. The relationship may even look perfect to outsiders. The tactics and interplays between the gaslighting, idolizing, head games, lies, and manipulations are not easy to see, read, or understand. What is happening to me?!?

Out of both marriages, for me personally the covert narcissist is the most dangerous.

Now I understand how relentless the universe must be in bringing back our inner trauma. Knowing and seeing the red flags is not enough. Rehashing their qualities does nothing but increase the idea we are powerless victims. The mentality it's "us versus them" divides us from the potent messages they send. These are the most important factors we have to recognize. The narcissist is the messenger to where the healing must be done. Seeing my trauma and tackling my issues has been my only saving grace.

I'm not making health claims here just sharing my story and experiences. That does not mean this will be your experience. It is just letting you see into my journey. My health has significantly improved since I started healing mentally and emotionally through the relationship dynamics. I know that probably doesn't make sense right now because so many counselors talk about going "no contact" or walking away from the relationship. My approach is revolutionary as it uses the relationship as a road map to see where you need to heal.

To make a long story short by the age of 25, I had my first experience with going into anaphylactic shock. In case you don't know what that is, it's an extreme allergic reaction where you have difficulty breathing, hives, and over all the worst icky feeling ever. It was right around the time I started dating my second husband. I had always struggled with some allergies but they had gotten progressively worse. At this time, I was still prescribing to the American health care system.

I was given a shot of epinephrine and a prescription for a steroid. I could only be on it 10 days or it would mess up my hormones. My skin rashes cleared up and I felt amazing during those wonderful days. It turned everything around for a small window of time. This didn't last though and I found myself living on Benadryl. They did tests, lots of them. Why and what is creating these allergic reactions?

Time rolled on and I went through the mysterious world of unexplainable health issues. The suffering is what sent me looking for alternatives. Modern medicine had let me down. I went through two more pregnancies and this took another toll on the body. Plus, the love bomber had been putting me through the confusing world of a covert narcissist. The phases of discard and devalue got longer while the love bombing showed up less and less.

At this time, I was clueless that any health issues may have anything to do with the narcissist. In fact, I had no idea what one was or what tactics were being used. I didn't feel good but didn't know why. Being sick with a host of things meant rounds of antibiotics wrecked my entire gastrointestinal track. I started to study, learn, and understand that the American diet was designed to foster sickness and went to natural alternatives. These switches in my diet helped but it was not the "cure all" I was hoping would happen.

That's when I started having experiences with feeling energy and consciousness. A whole new world opened up to me. Then the term narcissist fell into my lap and a healer named Melanie Tonia Evans. Her blog posts and YouTube videos were a godsend. I started piecing everything together. The experiences with feeling energetic shutdowns while being triggered into my trauma by my husband made the circle complete. I thank God/Creator/Source every day for opening me up to these experiences.

Once I googled health issues and the narcissist, I realized other people were talking about these same things. Yet, no one had step by step instructions on exactly what we needed to learn, heal, and evolve. The direct correlations between the physical, mental, emotional and energetic/spiritual body were ambiguous. Go no contact. Run as fast as you can. In my heart and soul, I knew that wasn't the answer.

I started to look at my covert narcissist in new ways. More like a personal trainer. I knew that when he ran over me with the gaslighting, blanket generalizations, and other crazy making behaviors my energy shut down. But if I stood up for myself, voiced my opinion, and stood my ground my energy opened up in beautiful ways. A set of spiritual tests became apparent that only he as my soul mate could supply. Finally, I was connecting the dots and my health was showing up for me. Not just physical but emotional, spiritual, and mental health.

Now, I'm happily married to the covert narcissist only because I have evolved. He is full of unhealed wounds and trauma, but honestly it used to match mine. I knew I could not keep running or avoiding the inner work and I didn't want to split my family up. That's why I took on the decision to engage peacefully. However, being peaceful and being a doormat are two different things. I had let these personality types run over me for too long.

The inner questions began. Are you going to let this person dominate you with their tactics OR empower yourself to see through them? I know that's not what you've been reading as everyone advocates go "no contact". Well, I disagree. I believe in going "no energy" regardless of if you have physical contact or not. People can drain you without them being around. So many victims walk away to find they still have to deal with the narcissist, if they have not healed it is brutal. The same suffering, they wanted to escape, is still there in a new way.

That's why getting empowered, educated, and taking steps to heal is the only way out. That means getting to know all the animals in "The Jungle". The exact personalities attracted into your life are key players. They show you where you need to strengthen and develop the one person this is all about. YOU! Until then, you cannot escape from them as they have a pivotal role in your life.

What we are truly seeking to avoid by going no contact or running away is parts of ourselves we don't want to work on or completely know how to. We self-avoid by eating, sleeping, working, alcohol, drugs, or some type of addiction. What else are we supposed to do? No one is breaking this down accurately. I clearly define those concepts in the chapters you are about to read. You will now know what to do.

Face yourself and the "crazy maker" head-on. See how they have the keys to every broken piece of you. These unhealed traumas desperately want recognition and soul evolution. That is the only way "out". We have to heal every single element of ourselves that allows us to get hooked so that we can stop the cycle.

When their imbalances, weaknesses, and dysfunctions no longer match ours, a fascinating thing happens. There is nothing in the relationship for them to get from us, and they go away on their own. We do not have to do anything other than show up as the healed and evolved version of ourselves to make them go running. If there is an inner locking of our relationship where we still must work, live, or be together, they do not bother us. I don't care where you find them — work, family, friends, or what life situations come up.

This takes deep personal work. A driving desire to end all the inner qualities that make the "soulmate" relationship stick like glue. Until you do your healing work, you become trapped here in the same repetitive patterns rolling around over and over, time ticking yet standing still. You may recognize this immediately as patterns from a parent that created deep trauma. Some circus of events occurs and it reminds you of being a child, except you've got a new parent. They resurface in a soul mate partner or marriage relationship.

There are several steps that we need to take together as you understand this revolutionary new way of seeing narcissists. This book will introduce you to concepts you have never heard of before. You have to take responsibility for the dynamics. Learn what to do about them. Why they keep showing up is unveiled as I explain the steps you need to take in detail. Revolutionary new concepts create a whole set of epiphany moments. It is possible to walk through the jungle of life and personalities without falling into any traps. This is an epic experience.

Imagine that! No matter what personality you're cornered into dealing with, you no longer go up and down like a Yo-Yo. No more emotional puppets played like a wrecking ball. Now you can look at people, relationships, and life in new ways. Use their behaviors to get stronger. Grow through your pain! I will show you how to see, work through, and use these relationships until you reach a beautiful space in your life.

There's no longer any emotional or energetic reaction to having a relationship with a narcissistic, controlling, manipulative personalities, or anyone else.

That's when you can start growing and learning about yourself and others. Be ready and willing to do the inner work. Allow yourself to get out of a victim mindset, which I've been there. I spent a lot of time stuck in this "poor me" attitude. Continuously running repeat victim stories in my head and to others of their callous offenses. Yet that solved nothing.

Ah, so much I didn't realize. There's a real battle here on Earth between good and evil. I am stuck in the fighting ring. Yet, I received no training what-so-ever on any of what I'm about to tell you. We are in an emotional war zone. Seriously! Unarmed with no weapons, no skills, no master strategy, or idea how to come up with one.

Who jumps into the boxing ring untrained and expects to know how to win against a trained fighter?

We all do unless we choose to get educated. What is the toxic person's strongest punch I need to block? What's their angle of attack? How are they trying to get in my head? Where am I leaving myself open to take that right hook? If you were a fighter getting into the ring, wouldn't you study your opponent? You really move into a warrior mindset ready to learn, heal, and grow from the experience.

Just think, if Earth was full of loving, caring, and happy people, we would never have to push out of our comfort zones. The most difficult positions in your life can either strengthen or destroy you. I just never understood the concepts and principles or their role in developing me. Dealing with negative energy and the complex system of manipulations was baffling. Even though I read the ideas from different experts and healers on the subject, I was missing an essential link that kept me suffering in the relationships. Something that I did not realize I also needed to master.

Get ready to go on that journey through this book. Let's identify your personality traits, the narcissists, and how these wheels work together. If you are educated on the tango between Empaths and Narcissists, skip to Chapter 3 on Self-Realization. No need to keep rehashing information you already know. Get to the new concepts right away. Going from powerless to powerful is the best feeling ever.

What parts of ourselves are reflecting through the narcissist or toxic personality we finally need to heal?

How is their trauma a match for our unhealed wounds we can resolve?

Is narcissistic supply truly what they have taught us to believe?

How do we look at our lives as a mirror and become responsible for its reflection?

What exactly does complete evolution mean, and how do you accomplish this mission?

Underneath these layers of the narcissist and you are two deeply wounded individuals. You are both seeking love and validation even if it's through complete opposite systems. Be grateful as you can ultimately see your inner wounds, faults, and not only heal but be compassionate with others. You need every single element of the narcissist. They are designed this way on purpose. When you move beyond the finger-pointing and blaming into asking yourself a new question…

What are the weaknesses, insecurities, and qualities in me that attracted the relationship?

This is a crucial link missing from healing from abusive relationships. You attracted the narcissist according to your inner wounds. We realize these personalities are the exact trigger people needed. They become our messengers through the pain. I honestly used to believe I was so angry with the narcissists in the outside world.

As I started using their qualities to do deep personal work, I realized I wasn't angry with them. I was mad at myself. I wasn't sure how to deal with this personality. I fell into their trap repeatedly, and I knew it. But then I didn't know how to get out or see that sucker before they clamped it down on me. I recognized I was in a repeat pattern with men. After leaving one narcissist, I married the next level, "covert narcissist". The similarities in the life situations and their personalities are so strikingly alike that I knew it wasn't about them. The universe was trying to send me messages through the relationships. Instead of running, I moved entirely into the situation with the heart of a warrior, healer, and lover. That's where it all begins no longer wanting to be a victim or stay in your repeat patterns!

The pursuit of happiness, strength, and growth through narcissistic, controlling, and manipulative relationships can finally begin. You are on an exciting journey. I'm happy to see you taking control. When you apply what you learn in these pages, no relationship or life situation can penetrate your inner peace.

Until then, there's no escape from the jungle. You know where you are…

CHAPTER 2
THE PLAYERS

WHAT QUALITIES ARE we talking about with the narcissist? How do we know we are in a relationship with one? What kinds of tactics are they using to control us? There are warning signs we can recognize later as the "new" wears off, but initially, it can be so hard to see them. These people are talented and skilled at creating illusions. We are mostly innocent and naïve, so we don't see it coming. You get caught in the trap by the time you put everything together!

Here's a more in-depth look at the qualities of a narcissist:

Charming: No wonder we can get hooked in when they can be so dazzling. They can make us laugh, shower us with their wit, and sparkle. When they are on their game wanting to impress us, they are the most amazing person you have ever met! Here is a link to my YouTube video explaining why the creator makes narcissists charming and good looking. Click here to be directed from the e-book: https://www.youtube.com/watch?v=sNQ9yRQK3oM

Telepathic: Narcissists are powerfully skilled at knowing what you want to hear. They can figure out people in a matter of minutes. I'm always amazed at how they know the exact amount to give to keep taking, taking, and taking. When you're just about to walk away from them completely, they tell you what you need to hear. Strange things happen, you call each other at the same time or have matching thoughts. There is some type of connection beyond the physical happening.

Conceited: They are very impressed with themselves but can appear quite humble to gain admiration. Honestly, at the heart of their actions, they feel superior, more knowledgeable, and smarter than others. They magnify everyone's faults while they elevate their abilities, talents, and skills. Conversations with them fall into two main categories. Ridiculing others and amplifying their weak spots or inflated stories of their hero-like behavior. All of this usually involves a game of lies and manipulations often appearing humble and modest even. "I'm not good looking." Or "I'm not that smart." Yet, you should be there attentively listening and clapping for them. They make sure you take their advice and directions above anyone else's, even your gut instincts.

Lacks compassion: Oh, narcissists can appear to be compassionate to lure us in. A covert narcissist will be fantastic at looking selfless and concerned about others. However, it's a lot of smoke and mirrors. They really cannot register what it feels like to be someone else. It's frustrating. The lack of concern for others is challenging to understand, whether it's at work, home, or in an outside relationship. Narcissists are the self-centered priority above anyone else.

Entitlement: They genuinely feel like they are unique, and that requires a higher level of treatment. You should give more love, admiration, material possessions, and ego feeding to them. In their minds, they are smarter, work harder, have higher-level skills, and deserve more than anyone else.

Fake Generosity: Narcissists know they need to appear giving to keep up their illusion with others. You'll watch them pay the entire bill at a big social dinner. While privately, they mock and shame you for every dollar you spend. They will buy expensive top of line items while you scrimp and worry about how much you spend on necessities. If your boss is a narcissist, you'll watch them spend a fortune on things they want. Yet they complain money is tight and profits are low if you ask for the pay you deserve or a raise.

Manipulative: Most of us want genuinely giving and loving reciprocal relationships with people. Narcissists surround themselves with anyone they can take advantage of or supplies them with their needs. They are great con artists — the ultimate salesman delivering a lot of fancy promises and illusions. Yet, there actions and words never match. You just signed up unknowingly for the use and abuse program. All because they are masters at manipulating situations and people.

Unrealistic: They have projects, ideas, and put pressures on you that are way beyond any human being. Reality is not a part of their mental makeup. If you see through their tainted illusion, pointing out their faults, or no longer fitting into the facade of their false personality, they have no use for you. If you stand against them, they will twist things to make you out to be the "bad guy." They have their version of reality and honestly believe it.

Liars: They have no guilt about telling lies or manipulating situations with false truths. Most of the time, this is pathological, as they distort reality to fit their needs. They also use lying as a tactic to get what they want. For example, in a romantic relationship with a narcissist, they will need to flirt with others to keep that ego inflated. Yet if you call them out on it, guess what?!? They will call you insecure, lie about situations, and twist things to make it look like you're at fault. Sometimes the fabrications will make sense to you, but other times, you won't be able to understand. Why would they lie about this? There is always an energy feedback happening either by pulling the wool over your eyes, frustrating, confusing, or shocking you.

Ultimate Victim: They are the wonderful person who is abused by others. Their childhood was traumatic, or they were dealing with mental, emotional, or physical issues they manipulate to gain attention. The poor me personality. You meet them, and they openly tell you their drama sucking you into the relationship. Once you are committed, you are now in the twisted reality. They will frame you to look like the self-centered, abusive personality while they are the innocent martyr.

Require The Center Stage: On a positive note, narcissists can be the most amazing, inspiring, and talented individuals. They need attention, the spotlight, and make great performers. There may not be the necessary follow-through to complete tasks, be consistent and accountable. These factors however do not discount their full belief in themselves and their abilities to "woo" the crowd. They can also be very inspiring leaders. However, when they are not the center stage, difficulties ramp up. Social situations that do not revolve around them always create drama. They can't have fun with everyone unless it's full of their fan club members. Be warned, if the narcissist cheerleaders are not present, some sort of tactics will be used to gain attention. They love pouting, disengaging with a lousy attitude, throwing a fit, or playing off some kind of sickness, so you have to go home. Holidays, for this reason, can be stressful. Narcissists don't realize that there's enough love for everyone. We can all win. Everyone in their mind is competition for attention.

Dr. Jekyll/Mr. Hyde: Can be loving and wonderful but switch unexpectedly to rude, ruthless, and cold-hearted. You cannot make sense of their behavior — one minute, you are cursing them up and down. You are hurt, shocked, ignored, or crushed by their behavior. Then they do something magically special for you, and you think awe they aren't so bad. I shouldn't be so hard on them. Without going in between these two different personalities, we would never continue relationships with them.

Hypocritical: If they make a mistake, it's acceptable, and they will pin someone else at fault. If you make that same mistake, they will inflate it and punish you. This could be in obvious ways, or it could be incognito. For example, belittling comments, jabs nicely concealed in a "joke," or even disapproving looks are standard tools you may not recognize.

Exploitative: Loves to act concerned to find out any internal weakness. Then uses that personal information to tear you down alone or in front of others. They can manipulate everything you say in confidence against you at one point or another.

Defensive: They cannot handle constructive criticism, yet they criticize constantly. You walk on eggshells to avoid hurting their feelings. Nevertheless, you can never judge what will accidentally set them off either. Getting your point across, being heard, or stating your opinion becomes so challenging because they are so over-reactive. Often making any statements or opinions against the narcissist triggers them into fit throwing, anger, rage, or the silent treatment.

Low Self-Esteem: They require constant validation, ego-boosting, and admiration. It can confuse people because they appear to be so confident and sure of themselves. However, that's just a superficial mask. Overt narcissists use bragging, boasting, and manipulating situations to make themselves a hero. Covert narcissists use fake humility to devalue themselves so they can hook you into giving them constant compliments. Propping up their fragile self becomes a full-time job and very draining.

Projection: Start paying attention to how narcissists outwardly blame, point the finger, and criticize you or others for the exact personality traits they cannot accept within themselves. If they over emotionally react to qualities in others and situations, it's a red flag. These are the exact qualities they have but cannot see, acknowledge, or accept. For example, if they are flirting with other people, they accuse you of flirting. You may in no way be flirting, but you are getting the riot act from them! It's not your actions they genuinely see. They are just blaming you for what they often do unknown to their partner.

Negative: It's challenging to pinpoint covert narcissists because they are so skilled at going between personalities. When they are the center of attention, they can be so funny and charming! Initially, you don't realize that they live in a negative cloud. As the new wears off, you notice they always shine a dark light on everyone and everything. All of these exaggerated worries, anxieties, and fears take over experiences. They can only fully support things that fit their illusionary world or inflate their ego.

Child-like: They are very much like a spoiled child. Anything that requires being a mature adult is outside of their primary skillset. If it needs them to handle a real crisis or grown-up issues, they falter. Although they are adept at figuring out who will carry the responsibilities for them, and know everything everyone else should be doing.

I'm keeping this list very basic and using a lot of generalizations. As we progress deeper into the heart of these relationships, we will unravel the parts of us that need all these narcissistic qualities. One of the biggest goals here is to move out of the old mindset that narcissists are the culprits of the world. In no way am I meaning to put them on the chopping block. We are just looking at the data and figuring out what spaces fit our situation.

We should all be grateful for the stage of naivetes, where we fall into their love bombing and idolizing. It means something beautiful for us. Those qualities we never recognized because we do NOT operate by that same navigation system. If we look at "projection," we can understand something genuinely healing. We see in others the qualities we have. If we don't lie and manipulate to get our way, then we assume others don't lie and manipulate to get their way. Narcissists have underlying qualities, and so do we.

I started to understand that I was something called an "Empath." If there is one word that opened huge doors of self-clarity, this is it. Exploring and understanding how you tick is just as important. You have qualities the narcissist saw as a commodity. They are very skilled at knowing who will be an excellent resource for them.

You have something they want, which could be a giving and caring personality that will cater to their needs. Perhaps it's materialistic, inheritance, financial stability, house, car, etc. You could be physically attractive, which will make others envious of their relationship with you. In a career, this could be a natural gift or talent at your trade. Skilled, hard-working, good-hearted employees, friends, or spouses are high assets to gain.

You have an incredible amount of compassion in your heart that allows you to see deeper into how others behave the way they do.

A skilled narcissist will look for a confident, independent, and reliable partner. They need someone who will tow the ropes of real responsibility in the relationship. Everything they are above dealing with you will handle.

People who are happy and positive in their lives regardless of needing much of anything are targets. As time goes on in the relationship, you notice feeling drained and empty. You may not recognize or know how this happened. Start "tuning in" and watching your internal register around people. How do I feel after being engaged with this person?

You give into other's demands quickly, forgetting your own needs, goals, and dreams. It is easy to give up what you want and revolve around what they want.

You don't enjoy being the center focus. They love the limelight and absorbing everyone's attention. In a sense, they are taking the pressure off of you while other people revolve around them.

Are you easily manipulated and controlled, fitting into their agenda and needs? You care about what others think, are non-confrontational, conform to demands, and that makes you shapeable into what they need.

Naturally blame yourself for your faults rather than others.

Naïve and gullible. You are a good-hearted person who wants to believe the best of others, so you don't see their tactics. You take what they say at face value.

Compassionate about others and their feelings, wants, and needs. You genuinely desire to help everyone.

Low self-esteem and confidence that is enamored by the narcissist's ability to shine under attention.

Co-dependency making it easier for the narcissist to take over as the center of your world. You need to be needed, so you attract the "needy."

We do NOT have a healthy relationship with ourselves. We lack internal strength, personal boundaries, and self-love.

Do you deeply connect to others' feelings and desire to help everyone heal? Whether it's on a personal level or the entire world, we genuinely want to save everyone and everything.

We say YES to others before we genuinely think of the consequences. We put other people and their needs before our own. The "takers" see us as a commodity. We end up in a lot of one-sided relationships continually giving.

We would rather shuffle our emotions and hurt ourselves, so we don't have to worry others. Narcissists are liars to hurt people. Empaths are liars to try to avoid hurting people.

People openly tell us about their problems. They know we are safe and genuinely care, which is an admirable quality as long as we set boundaries for ourselves. We do not take on their problems.

Emotional sponges and people pleasers make us feel drained by people. We feel better being alone and require periods of solitude to re-charge.

Being present in the now is difficult when you are deeply connected to the trials and tribulations of this world. Nothing here seems to fit in with who we are, so we check out. There are too many people hurting each other. There is too much hurt inside of us. It's painful to get in our body and honestly deal with being here. Besides, we feel so powerless about all of it! Day-dreaming, floating, or addictions become our coping mechanisms. This is precisely why it is easy to gaslight us because we are rarely fully present.

We connect deeply with animals, others, and the earth. The abuses of humanity hit our hearts. Rescuers! Activists! The narcissist is disconnected from empathy. We are over-connected.

Have a hard time fully relaxing with other people, as we are super sensitive to the feelings and thoughts of others. Negative thoughts from another person we can feel on a magnified level.

Identifying who we are requires self-realization as we are so open to everyone else. Finding our own authentic identity takes self-work.

We use several avenues to protect ourselves in a social situation. We can withdraw or become shy. That allows us to not engage in the hurt that seems to be passed around by people. We want to be social. Yet that means being involved in the ways the world is messy. There is this underlying competition going between everyone, and we do NOT want to be involved. Or we run around trying to please and make everyone happy all of the time. The social butterfly wants to keep the peace between everyone. Does everyone have everything they need? Are they having a good time? It's exhausting!

SENSITIVE to thoughts, feelings, energies, and the world itself, which we take on for ourselves. That makes the world draining, as all we see is suffering. Wars, pollution, homeless, starving countries, abuse to humanity… It's everywhere. We cannot fix, heal, and save everything and everyone.

We feel harmony in being in the great outdoors and with animals. There is a healing vibration in nature. The most significant advantage for us is that we escape from this complex web society weaves. Animals and nature do not have opinions, criticisms, or demands. They are "being" and loving unconditionally.

Those are some character traits that make us a magnet. Beyond those individual parts are the actual techniques narcissists use against us. We have no clue about these tactics because we don't operate like a narcissist or toxic person. They are using strategized moves to tear us down. Mastery of the inner workings is solid gold in your self-development. If we don't understand the crazy in the crazy-makers, we are leaving ourselves wide open for abuse.

So, what's inside the working of the narcissists' mind to "get in our head"? They have us playing like putty in their game of pain.

Idolize – Discard – Devalue: You will notice a cycle happening with the narcissists as they move you through different stages to get narcissistic supply. The idolize phase is the glory moment where we are the focus of their attention. Gifts, trips, sweet text messages, and thoughtful comments are all a part of this phase to "woo" you over. We find them a safe place to be in a crazy world full of hurt people hurting one another. These are tactics meant to hook you in and make the discard period more painful as you wonder what happened? They pull the plug and have no concern for you what-so-ever. You, as a codependent, will take their rejection personally and find it hurtful. Or you'll notice those loving comments turn into underhanded cut downs camouflaged as jokes or you're getting the silent treatment. Perhaps now you are on the back burner, and someone else is getting the "idolize" and "love bombing" treatment. Some head games are happening here on purpose. When you see how eloquently they move you through the cycles, it is mind-blowing!

Projection: Be prepared to be accused of everything they are guilty of doing. Your rational mind cannot understand the accusations. Why would they think that about me? Guess what they are guilty of those exact behaviors. Their guilt is showing up! Projection is an essential beauty of the ego that we all need to understand, not only because narcissists do it, but because we do it too. When people accuse us of things that we are not doing and will not let go of their constant, repetitive attacks, it's because they are guilty. What they are attempting to blame you for they do! For example, they don't respect or value you. Watch it come out as, "you don't respect me or appreciate what I do for you." Start thinking backward. Is this really what I do or what they do and are guilty of but cannot accept responsibility?

Victimization: The narcissist can turn every conversation around to make themselves the victim. They will lead you in circles until you are convinced. Everything is your fault. If you become upset by their actions, they are masters at twisting the situation to peg you as guilty. They will never fully give you any validation on your feelings, thoughts, opinions, and real problems. When you genuinely need them, they won't be there for you. They are most likely twisting stories and spreading lies about you to others to make it look like you are not supporting or loving of them. Yet, that's the furthest thing from the truth. It's uncanny. The person you go out of your way for has twisted everyone's perspective.

Shock: The narcissist will do and say all kinds of things to make you flabbergasted. So many times, narcissists have told me about different things that I couldn't believe. I would even think to myself, why would they tell me that?!?

Intimidation: If you question their authority or go against the way they think, expect a big display of anger, rage, threats, and manipulations. You wonder why you ever voiced your opinion. In covert narcissists, this is not big and flashy but comes out as worries, anxieties, and fears. They go around and around with their nagging and whining until you wish you never opened your mouth in the first place. The need for control and dominance pushes their buttons into a heightened state of finger-pointing, projecting, victimization, and "gaslighting." If you are not aware of how to deal with this, your senses will become weakened. You will become flustered against their tactics. We dislike seeing anyone upset and truly desire for the entire world to be happy even if it means shuffling our feelings or opinions. The peacemaker within us gives in and walks on eggshells to avoid confrontation.

Switching Subjects: Narcissists are absolutely the best at turning the conversation around when you have them cornered. Have you argued to find yourself frazzled why the original topic was switched from the issue at hand to something you did a few years ago? You will get completely frustrated. The initial problem where the narcissist is at fault never even gets addressed. Guess what? They know your weak spots too. They'll hit some wounded part of your soul to shift the blame to YOU. That wasn't even your original issue!! It's so frustrating. At some point, you decide it's just easier to stop voicing your opinions. Nothing becomes of it anyways. The hammer usually comes down on something you were guilty of doing in the past. They will never be accountable and use re-directing the conversation to trick you.

Gaslighting: The narcissist loves this tactic. Slowly but surely, they'll start getting into your head. Whatever mistakes you make, they will add comments to shred your confidence. "You're such an airhead." "You never think things through." "You are crazy." What kinds of statements come to mind for you? They have ideas, projects, make decisions, and if they don't work out, they will blame you or anyone else. "That was your idea." When clearly you know, it wasn't. Or maybe you don't because you are NOT used to anyone lying about the past, so you question yourself before you do them. Before you know it, they will have you convinced you do not know what's best for you. You don't remember the past correctly. You don't know the facts. You are the crazy one.

Domination: Narcissists can dominate a whole room full of people. If they are not the center of attention, they will re-route the conversation to them. If that's not an option, they will pout or give the silent treatment. They will escape the function. They don't feel good or some fabricated drama where they are the victim to provide their escape from the situation. They are not interested in hearing your opinion or anyone else's. Besides, they know better than everyone else anyway. You notice that social situations that do not revolve around them become a "problem." Hobbies, interests, etc. must align with their needs.

The Silent Treatment: When you do not follow their ideas or visions of how things should go, they will give you the silent treatment. At work, you may question the narcissist decision, or you say no to an assignment because you're overworked by them already. The narcissist will punish you. Let's say you didn't switch over from call waiting to pick up their phone call. Maybe you stood up to them in dealing with one of the children. Perhaps you've done absolutely nothing. They want to make you feel you are insignificant and, in most relationships, they have isolated you from other healthy bonds. You are truly alone.

Love Bombing: This phase will show up initially to win you over and throughout the relationship if you pull away. What a beautiful and wonderful time you will be having. They will lavish you with love, attention, gifts, and charm. They know precisely how to be the perfect soul mate, friend, career opportunity, or dream situation. Narcissists can be very attentive and caring. This period in the relationship keeps us hooked into them. You will also notice it is the only time they may accept guilt, apologize, and be accountable. The love bombing is also always what we remember during the break-ups.

Isolation: They want to keep you all for themselves. If your energy and attention go to other's relationships, hobbies, careers, and adventures, they cannot be center stage. Slowly, they will put a wedge between you, your family, friends, and pursuits.

Triangulation: This is another sort of tactic that fits with isolation. Narcissists love to create triangles with people. They will have someone else who is easily moldable be their supporting friend. If you get in an argument, they will use this "other person" to get validation on their crazy-making. What happens when you are a bully? You need two or more people ganging up on one person. That way, they can seal off the deal. Look, now you are outnumbered. You must be wrong.

Warden Mentality: You can have these friends, go certain places, have these ideals, and they will be fully supportive of you in those spaces.

They can have free range to do as they please. You cannot have those same freedoms. If you do, they will make it a painful experience in some way.

Jealousy: They will be jealous but do not expect them to adhere to the same rules. Social situations become agonizing. "You're not paying me enough attention. You're having fun with your friends." It's a complete work out to go anywhere with them. In marriages, they can have friends and often flirt unknown to you. Meanwhile, you can't even be courteous to others without getting the riot act! Friendships with them are exhausting. They see everyone else as the enemy. You will see lots of comments coming from them to persuade you against healthy relationships. As a peacekeeper, the path of least resistance looks like distancing yourself from others. You will dread going places because you don't want the drama. "You said the wrong thing. You stood too close to someone. You shouldn't have told them that."

Smear Campaigns: Narcissists love to pinpoint an Empath and start twisting lies about them to make them look bad. If you go against the narcissist, you will be a victim of a colossal smear campaign to make sure everyone thinks you are at fault. If you go up for a job promotion and one candidate is a narcissist, they will use every low ball move possible to make you look terrible. They love to twist situations to make you look like the bad guy. Besides, they need to paint the illusion of their victimhood. Lies, manipulations, and stories must be fabricated to make sure everyone thinks you are wrong. You are a terrible person. They will target your friends and family as the number one audience to win with their smear campaign. That way, it will hurt you the most. Your friends and family aren't even on your side. And remember they are very believable. You fell into their trap once too!

Underneath these layers of the narcissist and you are two deeply wounded individuals. You are both seeking love and validation even if it's through complete opposite systems. Be grateful as you can ultimately see your inner wounds, faults, and not only heal but be compassionate with others. You need every single element of the narcissist. They are designed this way on purpose.

Let's untangle this mess of what we need to do so we can move beyond attracting them.

CHAPTER 3
SELF-REALIZATION

FIRST OPEN YOUR eyes and get accountable for how our personality disorders fit so perfectly into the narcissists. I know we don't want to accept that we are a match. On a personal note, there are so many nights I would wake up in that mid dreaming mid awake state with this horrific feeling. I couldn't open my eyes. It was so intense I would wake myself up freaking out. Even then it would seem like forever before I could actually get my eyes to open, although I'm sure it was just moments. I think lots of times the universe/creator/God is trying to communicate messages through dreams.

I ended up having to admit that I did not want to wake up to the truth about narcissists or myself. I wanted the fairy tale illusion to continue on so I could stay in the miserable comfort zone. I was avoiding reality just as much as the narcissist. I wanted to sugar coat my life and keep up the lie. I certainly didn't want to start inspecting into myself. Yet, our internal working orders fit together perfectly. My gears worked with his gears and if something didn't change the combination we were just going to keep going around and around and around. This is how people stay in patterns with narcissists for YEARS.

The child has unresolved issues with a narcissistic parent and then those trauma's move onto a new person. They maybe at work or a soul mate or a child but they will show up somewhere. I was done running and ready to face them and myself head on. Then I started to notice things.

He constantly required attention and validation. I got my self-worth from being needed.

He was extremely jealous, but it made me feel loved even though it was dysfunctional.

He loved being the center of attention, I had no clue what to do with attention. Being with him let me meld into the scenery, while he took center stage.

He lived in an illusion of himself that revolved around good looks, charms, and a fake reality of his superior abilities. I was easily disillusioned, naïve, and gullible. I believed and fell into his masks.

He never settled for less than the "best" while I second rated myself and would go without so others can have more.

He was completely unable to feel compassion for others while I was overly compassionate.

Those are just a few examples of how we can magnetically lock up together. The imbalances show us the essential elements of ourselves. This self-examination through our relationships with others gives us a platform to do self-work. I believe we are in a new age. All the finger-pointing we used to do about "them" we will start turning around to focus on ourselves. Relationships are really mirroring one another; the imbalances are where we have suffering.

We could use some of their qualities and they could use some of ours. At the heart of the opposing qualities is a similar matching inner wound. Who knows in some ways you may find you carry the narcissist quality and your partner has the opposite imbalance? Every single one of us combines ego (narcissists) and spirit (empathy) consciousness. We all have self-work to do, and that is the reason we are here in this place called planet Earth. There is so much to learn from the darkness outside of us to show us the darkness within. And once we shed light on it, heal, evolve, and grow from our suffering, the need for it can disappear.

For so long, they have taught us that everything is about the outside world. Things are happening "to us." It's not true. The outside world mirrors back the soul lessons, growth, and development experiences we need. This takes a genuine shift in beliefs. We must move fully from blaming, pointing the finger, and thinking everything is about them to the new age. Everything in my life is a reflection of ME. All suffering is designed to teach me something, and until I learn its message, I remain its prisoner.

In the examples, we are looking at opposing qualities that make "opposites attract" necessary. It's not a blaming perspective or labeling. We need all kinds of different combinations of people in life to develop and balance ourselves. Both narcissists and Empaths have strengths and weaknesses, designed to be great teachers for each other.

No one here is better or worse than another. We are all reflected energy from the same source wired in ways necessary to use our relationships with one another to build, heal, and evolve ourselves. This book is as much for narcissists looking to work on their issues as Empaths. It does not matter. Your personal decision and ability to take action to be the best version of yourself is the only thing you need.

Some keys to seeing and testing yourself:

Look for emotional "triggers" meaning everywhere you over-emotionally react to the qualities in someone else is a key. Our hang ups, strong negative feelings or repeat victim stories are keys. Anywhere you get hung up obsessively about someone or have an over-emotional reaction; there are lessons. We all "project", meaning we rant and rave about the issues other people have that we actually have ourselves but do not want to see, acknowledge, or accept. Narcissists are not the only ones who project. Start unraveling if this is something you do that you cannot see or an unbalanced part of yourself that they are triggering?

If you have decided that it is not a "projection" or judgment of something you are guilty of ask yourself this question. Is this somewhere I am out of balance? The narcissist is a bully and I am a doormat. Until you can stand for yourself in an evolved way you will attract bullies and then get emotionally worked about it. These are called triggers. They are keys that must be investigated.

Start observing yourself from an outsider perspective. When you meditate, shower, or are sitting idle, use visualization to picture yourself. Add a new twist. Put yourself in the body of someone you don't like. Behave like you think you do but add in that element of being in a different body. That way, you can be more objective about yourself.

Another idea is to ask other people you trust their opinions. Do I do this? Do I behave like this? If you have several different people all saying the same things to you about your qualities, take note.

Look for repeat patterns where you feel like you are in a hamster wheel doing the same things over and over. For example, I keep dating these same personality types. Or I keep landing these jobs that pay nothing while I slave away my life. Even if you leave the situations keep popping up with the same underlying problem. The people may change or life situations but it's that same issue presented in a new way over and over.

ASK FOR THE UNIVERSE TO SEND YOU MESSAGES. The universe and life are always communicating with us. Opening our eyes to its beautiful design and how it tries to show us things all the time is mind-blowing. It just takes a shift in your awareness.

Most Empaths are very unaware of who they are at their core. It takes looking within and connecting back to ourselves to figure out… who am I, what do I like, and what do I really want to do with this precious life? As you look into these items really start looking into YOU. Assess what you need to work on and give yourself a rating.

#1 - I DO NOT LIKE BEING IN THE CENTER FOCUS. (Insecurity) attracts I MUST BE THE CENTER FOCUS (false confidence)

Narcissists are fantastic at being in front of people because they live and feed off attention. They are perfect in their own eyes plus confident in their abilities. Even if it's their illusion, guess what? They will shine under the spotlight while you worry about putting one foot in front of the other. You're so focused on what everyone is thinking about you, feeling uncomfortable, or so insecure that you can't fully be in your body when all eyes are on you.

Start doing self-work to become more comfortable in your own skin. As Empaths, we are very sensitive to criticism. Being in front of people creates an insecurity. Especially if we are with narcissists who always blow up our mistakes, it makes them feel more secure if they can laugh, mock, and shame you. They delight in finding your every weak space and pointing it out. This creates anxiety and trauma in our bodies. We run from being the center focus to avoid criticisms.

Do some self-inquiry on how comfortable you are in different situations. If you need the center stage, then ask yourself why you have difficulty sharing the "limelight"? Or vice versa, if you dread public speaking or getting out in front of people, start asking yourself why and how you need to work through this area. We are looking to attain balance here of being able to rock center stage or be the best back-row cheerleader depending on the situation.

Truly, the narcissist's ability to shine in the limelight is something we admire about them. When they are on their game wanting to impress, they are full of entertaining commentary, sparkly shows offs, funny, and charming. We are happy to let them have the whole show. It makes us feel more comfortable. They create a safe space for us to interact without having to be the center focus.

It's only our egos that rate, compare, and judge us. We are just as capable as the narcissist at rocking center stage. We have just lost that element of ourselves as we became molded by our parents, society, and wanted to please those around us. As you heal and evolve through this, you will see your personality come back again. You will realize once we get over our insecurities, the thing that threatens the narcissist the most is you being you. Don't worry you may be unaware of who you are yet and that's ok. Connecting back to yourself will happen as part of the process.

Doing self-work allows several things to happen. Regardless if you are or are not getting the attention, it is irrelevant to you. You continuously operate in your true authentic self. When you get ridiculed by others, it does not affect us the same way because we have done the inner work to heal our negative inner voice and self-criticisms. We will talk about this more in the next chapter called "The Mirrors."

#2 - In a narcissist's mind, nothing is ever their fault. They are perfect in every way. For an Empath, everything is their fault. They are incomplete in their minds. Both parties are completely out of balance. If you imagine a teeter-totter, the Empath is on one end of the spectrum while the narcissist is on the other end.

Neither of the two can identify:

WHAT IS MY PROBLEM?

WHAT IS THEIR PROBLEM THEY ARE
TRYING TO MAKE MY PROBLEM?

AM I ASSUMING THAT MY QUALITIES ARE
THE WAY EVERYONE OPERATES?

ARE THEY ASSUMING THAT THEIR QUALITIES
ARE THE WAY EVERYONE OPERATES?

For the narcissist, they have some qualities they have identified as unacceptable. They cannot be responsible for their faults, weak areas, insecurities, or personality flaws. This becomes a jealous partner accusing the other party of flirting or infidelity when it's really their own guilt. They are the one flirting or having extramarital affairs.

This can happen in an opposing way too. We project our qualities on the other party. We do not lie and manipulate to get our way so we don't see that coming from someone else. We genuinely want other people to be happy, so we don't imagine other people want us to be unhappy. We are not full of head games, so we don't realize when someone is playing head games with us.

It's so healthy you've decided to get educated. Separating "projection" is a key to letting go of a lot of issues that are not yours. When a narcissist and empath are both projecting these opposite inner qualities on each other without being able to separate whose issues are whose, we have a recipe for suffering. Start looking at your interaction with the narcissist. Examine and identify where are they projecting their blame? Then we can stop taking on their problems. Think about this like soul junk. They need a dumping ground for their inner garbage. Empath's so nicely put their loving hands out. In the end, we are holding our issues plus theirs.

Then it gets so heavy, we feel deflated and exhausted even though we can't pin point why.

There are a million ways this can manifest in life with a narcissist. For example, the narcissist whines, "You never do anything for me." In reality, they do nothing for you. They are trying to transfer their GUILT onto you. We project our good qualities onto the narcissist. We don't believe that people will lie intentionally to hurt us or shift blame because we don't deliberately lie, harm, or move the responsibility onto others.

We don't understand the narcissist DOES NOT have the same qualities as we do because we project our qualities on them. The experience is painful for us as we question, why would they think, say, or do that? We become frustrated, heart broke, and try to make sense of the situation.

Have you ever had a relationship where you bent over backward for someone? You truly went out of your way to help them. When the shoe is on the other foot, and you need help, they are nowhere. That's because we are that friend who will be there for you. They are not that type of friend and do not have those qualities. We assume that they are, and when they do not show up for us, we take it personally. It hurts our feelings. We blame ourselves and think it has something to do with us.

When we fully understand the psychological dynamics of projection, we can now separate these issues. We do not expect people to treat us the way we would treat them. What's impressive is as you become better at understanding people, you realize exactly who is worth your time, energy, and love. Who just wants to use you? Plus, we no longer take on other people's blame by understanding the rules of projecting and seeing that this is their guilt showing up.

When they do not give back to the relationship in the same way, we have a new understanding. We are projecting how we would be in the relationship rather than the partner's real qualities. Now you see how you've assumed they would treat you the way you would treat them rather than seeing them for who they truly are inside. We can fully separate what is happening here rather than take it personally. You need to identify whose problems are whose and let's face it neither empaths nor narcissists are good at it, but we can strengthen our skills.

Start taking an inventory of everything the narcissist accuses you of and ponder for yourself. Is this something they are guilty of doing themselves and want to blame me?

Everyone in this universe is guilty of "projecting." You will see it as precisely what is triggering us into emotionally reacting to a situation. Go through a checklist with yourself when you get into a confrontation or situation when someone is pointing the finger at you, or you are finger pointing at someone else. Do I do this, and I cannot see, accept, or acknowledge it? And vice versa, are these accusations about me, or is this something this person does that they cannot see, and I shouldn't take it personally?

If they are accusing you of things you are not guilty of, you can be sure it's their guilt. They cannot help it and it is not you at all. That alone will answer many mysteries of their behaviors. Now you can separate whose fault is whose and stop accepting everything as your fault.

#3 - Not only does the narcissist blame shift, but they facilitate another system of smoke and mirrors called gaslighting. Gaslighting is a common technique where the narcissist lies about the past, people, or situations to create the reality that fits their version of themselves or what they want everyone to believe. I remember reading a blog post that was so spot on about the narcissist's skills on shifting the blame.

"I paid the electric bill the narcissist exclaimed as we all sat in the DARK." Giggles! Yes, my dear narcissist, it's everyone else's fault but yours. Really, the narcissist forgot to pay the electric bill. Oh, but wait, the narcissist doesn't make mistakes. Instead of being accountable, they make up their version of reality. The electric company is at fault. Or maybe they start blaming you, professing they told you to pay it when they never mentioned anything to you. Then they sell it to us through a technique called gaslighting. These lies and manipulations are an escape route where they blame other people for their faults, insecurities, and weaknesses.

What is our fault in this tango of lies and manipulations?

We doubt and question ourselves, making us an easy target. Most empaths are not entirely in their bodies. The world is too painful to deal with until we heal our broken parts. We mentally, emotionally, and spiritually check out a lot. Unfortunately, that may include trying to escape with drugs, alcohol, food, or self-abuse patterns. Regardless we are not fully present and are operating like robots, so we are more susceptible to being gaslighted. Have you ever been driving to get to your destination and then you wonder… did I stop at that light? Or what did I do yesterday? We are mechanically operating, but we are not fully present.

When the narcissist gaslights us, we are NOT sure?!?! What happened in the past? We doubt ourselves before we ever question them. So here they are leading us in loops about who we are, what we did, or how it's our fault, and we follow them. We aren't sure. Besides standing solidly in our version of reality with someone toxic makes a blow up happen. Anytime you have a different opinion from them be prepared to enter an emotional war. This makes us want to tip toe around them. It's just easier to keep your opinion to yourself.

Going along with them takes less thinking on our part plus no confrontation. The keep the peace personality inside of us would rather go along even if we know what is right. We don't enjoy arguing. IF we have created a situation where we make anyone angry, upset, or hurt, our immediate reaction is to feel guilty and retract. We have valid reasons, concerns, issues, or fears that need to be addressed. Yet we are too afraid to voice them. We take the blame over sticking up for ourselves.

Start taking notes on things. Get solid in yourself and reality. I have no doubt; you will be surprised. The master illusionist has disillusioned you much more than you realized.

At first, you are just getting present and paying attention. Next, you hit that space in soul development where you stand up for the truth. You may find the narcissist completely unable to see your perspective. They cannot look at the facts and agree. State your case and then "agree to disagree" with them. Hold your own opinion despite their arguments and viewpoints against you.

They love to pull the wool over our eyes. We have to stop letting them get away with it. Once you jump this spiritual hurdle of getting present to fight for the truth and voice it in a balanced way, they will have taught you many great lessons. You believe in yourself again. Now you are standing up for your opinion, dealing with confrontation, and agreeing to disagree if necessary. Which most likely will happen. The narcissist won't decide, "Oh, maybe you're right. I am wrong."

This frustrates some people to no end as they try to convince others they are right. Most narcissists will rarely agree with you, nor do they need to. If you want other people to honor your ideas, thoughts, and version of reality, be willing to accept theirs. When dealing with a narcissist, my favorite way to exit a conversation is to tell them I respect and honor your opinion. I have my own and do not agree with you.

Once you stop trying to convince them, show them the truth, or be connected to them "seeing it," you will save yourself a lot of wasted time and energy. It's not about them agreeing with you. It's about you seeing through the gaslighting, sticking up for yourself, and standing in your truth un-wavered by anyone else. Once you can accomplish this self-development, these situations will not bother you anymore. You are nothing more than grateful because you can see your personal evolution by their crazy-making behaviors.

#4 – Narcissists love to set the deck on their side with people who are their puppets. They usually have a string of people who live in their land of illusions and stick up for them. Honestly, let's face it. Anyone who doesn't live in the narcissist fantasy land must be cut out of their life. If the narcissist and empath are not both evolving and healing once their old tactics do not work, they will leave you. Or if you demand a mutual relationship where both parties contribute in equal parts, the disappearing act and excuse bus will show up. They do not keep friends who see through them or who do not serve them in some way. Everyone in the narcissist's life serves a purpose in feeding their ego or is some type of commodity.

They are skilled artists at reading people, knowing what they need to hear, and being the exact match. Therefore, they are great cult leaders like Hitler. They can mind warp and twist people's reality into a place where they follow them with uncanny loyalty. Plus, they make examples of anyone who tries to go against their philosophies by blow-ups, fit throwing, and keeping others walking on eggshells. That's exactly what a narcissist loves to do. Get a tribe of people they have completely disillusioned. Reward those who support and serve them while publicly punishing anyone who goes against them.

They love to use these outside people who are brainwashed by them as resources to validate themselves. If you are stating your own opinions about something not in the narcissist ideals, they bring in the "triangle person" or several outside people. They try to outnumber you. XYZ person agrees with me about this, and you should too. Or they use other people to threaten the person. I'll just call so-and-so right now so they can tell you fully knowing you don't want everyone drug into your arguments. They love drama. However, you do not and don't want the entire world knowing your relationship details.

Naive to the manipulations used against us attracts master manipulator of people.

If you are not programmable and go against this person's ideals, they get rid of you and twist stories to make you look like a bad person. This means that once you leave the narcissist, they will set up everyone against you and make themselves the victim. The smear campaigns start-up framing you. You must be solid within yourself. You are a good person despite what anyone else thinks about you. Other people will believe their lies.

They are professionals at the head games they play. Remember that you believed them fully. Their skilled illusions easily disillusioned you.

Now they have collected their followers and like a pack of wolves are circling stories to bad mouth you. Can you stand alone, and not be an emotional puppet to their attacks? Be honest, is this a weakness? You've never learned to be a solid sense of support to yourself. Are you sensitive to what others think about you? The people-pleaser isn't able to please everyone. Can you let go of your need to be approved of by others? Approve of yourself.

Lot's of self-growth can happen by the narcissist's personality traits.

#5 - Don't be angry with the people they make their puppets. I remember after I left my first husband, my mom would tease me. You drank the "Edward Johnson Kool-Aid". It was a joke, but it has a ring of truth to how we are to their real personalities — gulping down their brainwashing in the sweetness of the love-bombing. Everyone has done this or been blind to people. Just because you are awake doesn't mean you can't have compassion for others. You have been in their shoes and once skipped down the road to their fantasy land.

Besides, the narcissistic pack is allowing you to stop anyone from destroying you by their thoughts, judgments, or criticisms. No matter how many are in the pack of wolves, you remain solid in who you are and your sense of self. Triangulation and smear campaigns are by design to teach you real inner strength. Standing alone for what you believe in and knowing who you are despite the narcissist twisting everyone against you shows we have become a solid sense of support to ourselves.

FALSE SENSE OF SELF MEETS WEAK SENSE OF SELF

We have to stand in our truths and ideas of reality. If we are insecure or have any self-doubt, they will convince us of their ideas. When we fully commit to doing the self-work and realize that a narcissist is a tool for self-development, it creates a real sense of gratitude and unconditional love. Here you have to gain inner solidity. There is a newfound sense of confidence and strength by not wavering to other's games, manipulations, or lies. Besides, you may not have realized you were being lied and manipulated before. You were naïve and gullible, still following the narcissist pack and their false reality.

#6 - Now that you see reality clearly, you will have to face whatever repercussions happen from going against them and their puppets. Narcissists can be brutal, heartless, and insensitive when you break their idea of themselves and stand for the truth. They love to set examples using people to set the stage. They reward those who follow the regime. Others who do not go along with them are publicly punished, humiliated, or shamed. In certain religions or the case of Hitler or ISIS, this means execution. They use FEAR as a tool to dominate and control.

MANIPULATOR OF FEAR ATTRACTS
MANIPULATED BY FEAR

Narcissists are threatened by people who go against them. I mean really, what if you infect the whole tribe of narcissistic followers by standing against them? This can create an ugly situation as the narcissist feels fearful, insecure, and threatened by you. In their minds, they must punish you. Whatever you hold dear to your heart is a target for them. What will hurt you the worst? If it's your reputation, they will spread rumors and lie about you. If it's a business relationship, they will pull the plug on their end of the deal. If it's your children, they will intentionally play games and hurt them to get to you.

They do not have honest, sincere relationships with people. Everyone is viewed as a tool for whatever ways will benefit their purpose. Truthfully, you've hurt the narcissist deeply as they feel you have abandoned and betrayed them. Everyone is for or against them. If you do not believe and follow what their ego wants to think about themselves, this is ultimately painful and shattering to their world. You must be squashed in such a way they never have to see or deal with you again.

We have established we care too much about what others think of us. This provides us with the opportunity to break this inner insecurity. When standing in the face of false judgments, accusations, and lies, we must know regardless of what others think, who we are, and what we stand for. Now we have to step through fear of the outcome by fighting for our principles. They have carefully chosen the treasured items in our lives to use against us. We think we will lose whatever this may be for us if we stand up for ourselves. Picking faith over fear is difficult, and we must learn to step over the hurdle. This is precisely why they choose the object you fear losing or hurting the most in their games.

Children

Money

Security

What you are worried and scared to lose, they will painfully manipulate it against you. Yet, the fear is already inside of us and being attracted to the surface through the relationship tie. Having complete faith that being authentically you deeply entwined in your truth and what you stand for regardless of the consequences is an enormous spiritual hurdle that must be jumped.

When I would threaten to leave my first husband, he would first attempt physical entrapment. The next step would be to physically with hold my daughter. One of our greatest disasters was in this exact scenario. I threatened to call the cops if he wouldn't give her back to me. This triggered him as he had been through several run ins with cops in his past. We raced toward the only phone in the house.

Our 3-year-old daughter strapped to his hip as he tackled me over the couch. I landed on an old trunk we used as a coffee table. As we flipped over on the floor, he punched me with an open palm right in the nose. It broke on contact and started bleeding. We lived in an apartment and the neighbors heard the commotion. They came over to check on things and it was the only reason I escaped.

I went back to him to try and work things out after this encounter. He said he never hit me. GASLIGHTING technique. I had two black eyes and a broken nose. At another point he said that's how you kill someone. You hit them not with a fist but with the palm of your hand. SHOCK technique. I married someone who would kill me at the wrong provocation. Ever since then I've seen this re-occurring FEAR pattern in my life.

I eventually left him for good but married husband number two. The covert narcissist. Guess what his "go-to" move is as soon as things get heated. I can leave but I can't take the kids. Now he's not physically abusive, just emotionally and he knows that's my trigger. These men keep coming back to me on purpose so I can overstep my FEAR. This has happened already as I have overcome fear with faith. It no longer affects me. Now he no longer uses that as a playing card in disagreements, because I've changed and evolved.

I remember the epic day it happened. He said that I could go but couldn't take the kids. I didn't fight or push back. I agreed to it and stated my case. This would give me an opportunity to get on my feet. I have always worked for my husbands, in both marriages because it allowed me flexibility to be a stay at home mom. I pointed out how great this would be for me. Of course, the narcissists mind is reeling then because they don't want to actually help you. Changing the power and control dynamics besides overcoming fear has been an expanding experience.

Do you these reoccurring patterns hold us with relationships until we do the inner work. We attract what we fear so we can overstep our dysfunctional and abusive patterns. The bottom line is narcissists push everything we fear at us to test, strengthen, and finally stop manipulating ourselves with it. Plus, the experience is an excellent opportunity for us to read personalities, research people, and do some homework on them before we hand them our trust.

"Beware of false prophets, who come to you in sheep's clothing but inwardly are ravenous wolves." Matt. 7:15

#7- LIARS ATTRACT GULLIBLE AND NAIVE.

They are the sheep in wolf's clothing. If it wasn't easy to pull the wool over your eyes, you wouldn't feed into them and their lies. You wouldn't be a target. They do not engage or surround themselves with people who will not support their false reality of themselves or the world. Empaths are often way to open and giving. We do not keep secrets, and are terrible at surprises because we often blow it.

Narcissists are very secretive in their lives. Often living a double life. The one with the partner and the one with their outside sources. While the Empath is blabbing away all the details of everything, like I have $325,000 in my checking account and my social security number is blah, blah, blah with an excellent credit score of over 700. The narcissists taking notes, and keeping all their information under lock and key.

They want what you have, plus none of what they have will ever go towards you unless they are love-bombing. All of their relationships are with people that will give to their advantage. Time, energy, and resources will swing in their favor by all friendships, relationships, and business deals or they do not engage. It's also to their benefit to keep secrets so they can shock you, take you off your guard, and manipulate your emotions.

We are out of balance by being to open, trusting, and giving without doing the background research. Having relationships is challenging because all we attract are people who want to use and abuse us to their advantage. We need to balance ourselves, besides getting educated on spotting liars and manipulators.

Look for past incidents when they swear something didn't happen that you know it happened.

When narcissists want something from you, they will idolize and adore you. They plug into your needs, wants, and desires by being thoughtful and wonderful before something happens like you go out of town without them or they bought some big-ticket item for themselves with the family budget. Or they need you to do something for them.

They are a lot of fancy talk that sounds wonderful, but their actions don't match up. Do NOT listen to people watch what they do. Actions are where you will find the truth.

No matter what happens, it's never their fault. They usually have a couple of tactics to never be accountable. It could be switching the subject to something you did wrong and using it to make you feel guilty. Your valid inner concern never gets addressed as they lead you in circles. OR they look sorry and promise to change, which happens for a short period of the "love bombing" phase. Once you are back on their hook, the old patterns, lies, and manipulations come back as they "discard and devalue you" once again. They were never sincere in their promises. It's just our desire to want to believe them that is sincere.

They are full of ideas and ready to volunteer to be the great supporter of your dreams and goals. However, once you need help, they are not there for you. Excuses, stories, negative projections, groans, and the great talker show up.

Eye contact and tone of voice change can be significant indicators. When they are luring you in for the kill, they have a soft sensitive, caring tone along with eye contact and body language supporting they are interested in you. They are ONLY interested in you as a commodity. Yet, here we are flattered that someone cares about us, not seeing it as the con artist laying the trap. Start reading articles on body language indicators and watching the narcissist when you know they are lying so you can start reading people immediately.

Over bragging on themselves and all of their greatness is a clue. All stories paint themselves as the hero. They are happy to fill up all of your time with these grand inflations of their amazing displays of skills and talents while they belittle and pick apart others. We are just listening so attentively and admiringly. We are amazed with everything they do, shoveling in the bullshit like a big fancy cake. The "egomaniac" is on the loose but it tastes so good we don't know what's happening. Any time someone tries to over sell me on something I now question the motive.

If people delight in over-inflating themselves while criticizing everyone else, it's like a warning bell to run. A true empath does not like to hurt other people. They try to make the best of other people's faults. Usually, they are full of telling you their faults before thinking about anyone else's.

These are just a few ideas to get you rolling. When you are no longer disillusioned and see the warning bells early, you will be so grateful that you awakened. Your progress is nothing short of amazing!

#8 - An Empath is non-confrontational. A narcissist is highly confrontational and has a toolbox of tactics to make sure, if you go against their way, you will pay. Narcissists blow up, fit throw, and punish you for having a different opinion, following your ideas, or being uncontrollable. Empaths dislike people angry, hurt, or upset. They take those emotions on unknowingly as their own.

The Empath must learn to stand up for themselves in a healthy balanced way. Isn't life interesting as I think most of us who find ourselves in narcissistic relationships are trying to hide from the world of confrontation, bickering, and fighting? And guess what happens. We trap ourselves with what we are running from!

You think the relationship, career, or friendship is this safe haven for yourself. That's the "love bombing" attractor agent. They will take care of you, so you don't have to deal with this messy place called Earth. I used to hand over the confrontational stuff to others because they're good at it!

I want to avoid those places. Let them do the dirty work. Guess what pops up though that confrontational personality on you. So, you walk on eggshells. You don't want to make them angry. They are like a ticking time bomb, and you can never figure out what you are triggering to set that sucker off. You may mention something in conversation that you wouldn't think was a problem AT ALL, and they will go ape shit angry. All over some minor detail in life. Why? You have no clue. There you are though just stuck in the tornado, unsure what started this fiasco?

So, what does the Empath do? Try to steer clear of any situations that might lead to the narcissist blow up. Now, look at what we've done by cornering ourselves with the exact positions we hate to be in CONFRONTATION. And woo hooo guess what while we are still unhealed, they are massive controllers in our lives! Now we get to face that part of our wounded selves regularly — awe the world and your life is a total setup.

We are both out of balance. There's no way out but loving and accepting yourself as you are and then stepping into the battle of words to finally stand for YOU!

NON-CONFRONTATIONAL attracts
HIGHLY CONFRONTATIONAL.

EASILY INTIMIDATED attracts INTIMIDATORS

Don't be surprised when they get angry, twist things, or use several manipulations to try and sidetrack your new evolved self. Don't fall for it, remain calm and in control so you can effectively argue your point.

Ever since my awakening I've discovered my body was also an energetic being. When others wanted to fight, I hit the flight response. My brain would not work because my emotions would be a mess. That led to all kinds of circuitry not firing correctly. Later I could think of what I should have done or How I should react, but never in the moment. It was like my cognitive thinking skills just left the building.

I discovered a lady who could see the energetic field around the body and its fluctuations. If you feel like you have this same issue you may enjoy some of her techniques. There are scientific reasons that this happens. All the blood rushes from our brain and we cannot make good decisions or think efficiently. You can use energy medicine techniques to re-wire your responses. This one is called the neurovascular hold.

https://www.youtube.com/watch?v=kU3san9Z84U

These new skills may take time to acquire and use without getting emotionally worked up yourself. All steps are progress on the path. There will be lots of opportunities to keep working on it. Just keep moving in these new directions. At some point, confrontation will be handled with ease and grace even with the narcissist.

#9 - An Empath doesn't know who they are because they become everyone who they are around. Mainly because they like to blend in and do not want to create waves. The narcissist loves this quality! Whatever their hobbies or interests are, those hobbies and interests become your own. You delve deeply into becoming that ideal match, trying to fit them perfectly. Besides, it's nice because you don't have to make a lot of decisions.

They can define you without you having to think or do any real soul searching. It's so easy for you to give up what you want to do. For you, when others are happy, it makes you happy. The narcissist has learned how to give us "happiness candy" for being what they want. It all works together to show us our disconnection with ourselves.

When this character trait is out of balance, it creates the perfect situation for you to be easily molded. The narcissist is so controlling and manipulative that you make the perfect pawn in their game because you are out of balance. The puppet and the puppet master.

They are so good at sculpting people. Things you may not notice take over by putting little negative comments about people, ideas, and situations. Shaping you to who your friends should be and what hobbies you should have. "Happiness candy" handouts happen when you conform to their demands. Punishment for when you don't. You may be ignored, criticized, critiqued, or shamed for staying true to yourself. Subliminally or blatantly they carve you to their delight.

Ask yourself what if you wanted to get away for a few days without them? See your family or enjoy a hobby with friends. Would they pitch a fit? Decide they suddenly want to do something with you. Use the silent treatment, or blow up to keep you molded into their needs. They love to use their tactics to shape what you can and cannot do. We mold to the tactics. If you do something that makes you happy, they are wired to get upset on purpose. You have to develop a couple of qualities here that you are lacking.

Make yourself a priority. We put others on the pedestal and shuffle our own needs.

Finding who we are at the heart of our soul — no longer allowing anyone in our heads that will define that for us. We stop choosing to absorb ourselves in others, their needs, wants, and desires.

Setting boundaries, regardless of whatever threats or tactics they use to get their way.

You may have seen this relationship dynamic as love, or it fed your ego by the fact, they "need you". Awe, they love you so deeply that they want you all to themselves. Or they need you… you can't leave what will they do?

You may have to face several inner wounds. Perhaps you don't think you deserve to do something for yourself. You feel guilty if you make yourself a priority.

Lots of inner spaces to SEE and finally WORK THROUGH!

Really, the narcissist just wants to keep you under their thumb, but we have to step under it. You as an Empath must do your own soul searching and find out who you are in this world with no one else defining, controlling, or telling you what or who to be. And you must stand for yourself in those hobbies, career goals, friends, or family decisions. Make choices to support yourself. You are worth it. Fight for it! The narcissist will make none of this easy.

EASILY CONTROLLED ATTRACTS
THE MASTER CONTROLLER

#10 - Now here's a fun one that most people don't want to accept. We love pointing the finger at others where they are at fault. Guess what? Victimizers love victims and victims love victimizers! We love to complain and blame the narcissist for their abuses to others. We are getting feedback from being pitied and for others' sympathy for our situation. It's a tough one to recognize because we have very valid arguments for being stuck in a relationship with a narcissist. They give us non-stop ammunition for our pity party!

Start watching your conversations. How much complaining do you do about them? Can you stop? Are you the "poor me"? Is it because you are blame shifting? Rather than being able to stand up to them, you complain to others. That's safer than facing them, making them accountable, or standing in your power. There are so many ways our dysfunctional wheels fit perfectly into theirs. We have the power to transform every single one of these patterns.

VICTIM attracts VICTIMIZER

POWERLESS attracts POWERFUL

#11 – Narcissists love drama while empaths try to minimize things. In some ways this is what makes them fabulously exciting and great story tellers. For example, they didn't just drive home. On their way a crash happened and they had to held the cops pull someone out of a car that they just know was going to explode at any minute. Meanwhile the empath would answer the drive home was fine. That's it. No drama. Nothing exciting. Everything is just flat and melancholy.

This is why narcissists can attract huge fan clubs, beyond they are truly in love with themselves and thus attract those who are something more happens. Drama. Excitement. Big Plans. Being around them provides the empath with something to actually talk about and brings some kind of interest to the hum drum of life.

DRAMA QUEENS attract MINIMIZERS

We could have a very heavy conversation about what reality truly is when really, it's so different according to people's perspectives. Everyone is having an experience according to perspectives. If you sneeze in front of a narcissist you most likely have a deadly flu and should see the doctor immediately. While an Empath could be suffering with serious health issues and avoid ever getting medical attention.

In some ways this is a manipulation tool for the narcissist. The fabrication of things leads the empath to sympathize and give, give, give. For example, the narcissist is complaining of how they are broke and have no money. The kids are sick. The husband lost his job. In reality, the narcissist blew the whole budget on some eccentric item for themselves. The oldest child sneezed today. The husband didn't have to go into work because the machinery equipment needed repair.

In the life of an empath a real crisis situation could be happening and it gets minimized or never even addressed. You can ask an empath, how are you? The empath says fine. In reality they just went through treatment for breast cancer. They couldn't work for the last six months. They have been living on credit cards and seriously have no money. Yet, you would never even know because they don't want people to worry or stress about them.

Regardless of if you are the drama queen or the minimizer of issues it's a twisted reality. The opposite end of the spectrum but the same underlying twisting of the truth and life. When you start doing self-work you want to find the middle ground of being truthful and honest about your life. In relationships with covert narcissists many people do not even know they are dealing with abuse because of their twisted perspective to minimize real issues and problems.

#12 - Have you ever tried to make a plan with a narcissist? Oh, it is frazzling! They cannot give you a straight answer. You're playing a game of charades when all you asked was a simple question. What time should we meet? Can you make it? Oh, dear lord, getting a commitment from them is like pulling teeth. Plus, whatever decision is made is subject to change at a moment's notice. They love having control of the puppet strings on what we do or don't do. We are solid people who like a plan ahead of time. We want to know what's going on and when. Here we are cornered into depending on someone who cannot commit to anything. Or if they have a plan, they hide it on purpose. It's completely frustrating.

The narcissist is teaching us some valuable lessons. Stop waiting on other people to make a plan and make your own. If the narcissist wants to join us great and if not, oh well. When you stop waiting on them to grace you with some sort of decision and make your own decisions, you stop being angry with them. If plans are unavoidably hinged on them, you learn to let go and trust the universal order of things. Whatever is meant to be works out or doesn't. Our egos want to take control and not trust the divine order.

The two personalities collide:

CANNOT MAKE A PLAN MEETS WANTS/NEEDS/
LIKES OR DEPENDS ON THEIR PLAN

And the narcissist enjoys knowing they have control over answers you need and will purposely not give them to you. Until you reach this point of accepting the universal order of things and let go of being in control, they are here to serve as teachers. And these are all just some prime examples of where, why, and how opposites attract. Everyone's life and relationships are different. You will need to cater this to different ways the narcissist shows up… at work, as a narcissistic child, family member, friend, or spouse. The bottom line, however, is the same.

You attracted the exact person you need to balance your internal scale.

Can you see it now? All the ways we must be cornered in this whole fiasco to work out our unbalanced internal parts? I say that full of smiles too because you know what? That's a great moment of self-realization.

The most significant transformations occur when you get real with yourself. I love seeing where I am my own poison.

Every person on this planet has narcissistic and empathic qualities, so you may find out that in some ways, you are in a role reversal.

Now absolutely, we can do some real blaming here. Trust me, I've been in that boat just rowing against the current of life for many years. I understand that too well.

IT'S THEIR FAULT.

THEY DID THIS TO ME.

WHY CAN'T EVERYONE BE NICE?

But what would happen if you saw your inadequacies rather than focus on the narcissist? Could you balance the scales that have been tipped for so long if you got serious about seeing your faults and balancing YOU? Absolutely! What if you decided it was high time you got to know YOU? You worked on the one variable that you can change. This relationship can be a profound experience of self-growth. Allow it to show you where you need to do self-work to balance out your inadequacies.

I highly recommend starting a journal. The trauma in our relationship will continue to roll on. Even if we end this relationship, if there are elements left unbalanced, the new partner will show up to corner you into dealing with them. Ask yourself if you feel like any of these listed items hit home with you. When you genuinely heal these fragmented parts of yourself, you realize something very profound. Narcissistic relationships do not bother you. You sail through confrontation, set boundaries, see-through lies and manipulations, break the puppet strings, and recognize which people you wish to invite into your circle. Plus, you have the inside view on which ones are toxic personalities.

> *"All that was great in the past was ridiculed, condemned, combatted, and suppressed – only to emerge all the more powerfully, all the more triumphantly from the struggle."*
>
> *– Nikola Tesla*

CHAPTER 4
THE MIRRORS

IN SOME WAYS, our relationships show us our unbalanced parts. In other ways, they become a mirror. All the issues we can't see are staring right back at us. The narcissist plays an essential role in being the messenger. They have the opposite internal wiring to show us these areas.

You CANNOT attract someone who loves you
unconditionally, until you love yourself unconditionally.

You CANNOT attract someone who does NOT
make you feel guilty when you set boundaries if
you feel guilty for setting personal boundaries.

You CANNOT attract someone who will be supportive
of you when you are not supportive of yourself.

You CANNOT attract someone who is
giving, when you cannot receive.

You CANNOT attract someone who honors and
cherishes you, until you honor and cherish you.

The list could go on and on. We have the exact person in our lives who treats us according to how we feel about ourselves!! So now that we have accessed where we are out of balance, we can face this other element.

The exciting part of realizing these areas is that it puts us in control. We have the power to do the soul work. Once we heal at the core of our being, we can attract new partnerships built on our healthy relationship with ourselves.

Do the same thing with this chapter. Take a self-inventory and make your soul assessments.

#1 - The Empath already has a low sense of self-worth. They will frantically try to do and be everything the narcissist dreams and desires. The harder the Empath tries, the more the narcissist feeds off the relationship. The narcissist, however, will never be happy with you. All right, let me edit that just a bit.

They seem to know how to walk the fine line, giving you just enough attention to keep you as their workhorse. Yet, not enough to feel fully loved and appreciated. So, what's going on here? How could this be your problem? What's the inner wound we haven't identified?

We attract a relationship that matches our internal compass. You're just spinning your wheels with those projects at work or trying to make that impossible deadline goal. Maybe it's a parent. You want them to be proud of you, yet they never give you credit for what you do or contribute. You will never be or do enough for the narcissist. They only sprinkle in admiration to wheel you on their line. Keep you trying harder and harder!

Manipulators love people pleasers. People pleasers are looking for validation and love from others because they have not learned how to be a solid sense of support, validation, and love to themselves.

This matches the wounded Empath. You internally feel within yourself you are NOT enough. You would never keep a relationship, career, or however, this external situation manifests to make you think YOU ARE ENOUGH. Do some experiments with this. The next time someone tries to pay you a compliment, watch your reaction. Do you argue against them or accept their admiration with gratitude? Can you receive praise genuinely, or do you deflect the comment and push it away?

I AM NOT ENOUGH attracts YOU ARE NOT ENOUGH.

We are in a hamster wheel with the narcissist that cycle's around and around going nowhere. We try to become EVERYTHING that the narcissist could want to discover that they still aren't satisfied! This becomes deeply painful. We want everyone to be happy and dislike criticisms, arguing, or confrontation that seems to be caused in the narcissist's opinion by US?!?

Recognize the narcissist will never be happy with you. EVER. They are not happy inside themselves, making it impossible. However, you must still be accountable for having the matching inner wound. They are supplying you with the internal message of how you feel about yourself.

Your internal voice never gives you credit for what you do. You pick apart your every mistake and blow it out of proportion in your mind. You feel that you are not enough. We have to do the self-work here. Realize that you are enough regardless of what they say, do, or how they try to make you feel "less than." Use their qualities to assess hmmm is the way the narcissist is talking to me a match for the way I speak to myself or some internal self-anger, guilt, trauma, or shame? Narcissists are skilled in finding internal soul wounds. They are wired to bring these painfully to light.

#2 - Let me explain how this works. There is another mirror where the narcissist is intentionally trying to break us down by working on us from two angles:

- picking at our internal weakness
- not validating us in our strengths, accomplishments, and achievements

This is the exact match for how we treat ourselves. We have a negative, self-critical inner voice that blows up our imperfections while never giving ourselves credit for what we do.

The narcissist is also using the reverse actions to build themselves up:

- not acknowledging any of their internal weaknesses and blaming others for their faults
- inflating their strengths, accomplishments, and achievements

They will criticize, mock, and scoff all your imperfections while never giving you any credit for your strengths. Maybe you just reached some major accomplishment, but they can't provide you with one approving comment. A high five. Something rather than being ignored. It's like a loaded gun is fired right into that space, begging to be healed. We over-analyze and self-critique our weaknesses while not giving ourselves credit for our strengths, contributions, or talents.

When they try to jump in your space and make you feel you are not enough, see how it feels in your body. What emotions do you feel? Are they the messenger to you? They are painfully pinpointing, where YOU do not think you measure up.

Would it be painful anymore if you realized you are enough? If you knew it was ok to make mistakes and be imperfect, would you shrug off their grinding comments, disapproving looks, or "jokes" that are jabs? You could have them pointing their firing gun at you and be unaffected. If you use this as a tool to see all those places you love you on conditions and heal, they will strengthen you!

The tactic works well for them. The narcissist tears you and others down, so they can keep up the illusion they are superior. You have to be squashable to fit the mold. Those people who are confident in their abilities and have deep self-love regardless of their imperfections blow narcissists off. Anyone in their circle who doesn't fit these fundamental requirements is threatening to them.

They can't stand to share the limelight, even if being the "top dog" requires twisting, slandering, and manipulating things. In work situations, it's just as frazzling. The office narcissist is blowing up any mistakes you make and exaggerating their minor contributions. For icing on the cake, they twist everything to make you look bad. You better get into the fighting ring of life or you are going to be their favorite snack.

It's on purpose and intentional. Until you find this grand key, it will create suffering for you. We cannot understand that some people are envious and jealous of other people's achievements and strengths. We admire others who have the qualities we don't have but would love to develop.

That leaves us wide open for being psychologically screwed with because we don't have those qualities; we do not see them.

The underlying issue in our soul map is that we have never learned how to be our source of love, approval, and support. We can't give ourselves credit, so we attract people who don't give us credit. We inflate our imperfections in our mind, and so does the narcissist. They are wired the same way we are wired until we heal, up-level, and evolve.

We need to balance our internal scales. Recognize yourself in your achievements. Say them out loud and be proud. Work on your weaknesses and insecurities, but don't inflate them in your mind. Create a balance and realistic ideals between your true qualities and others.

Guess what happens when you validate yourself rather than depend on anyone else. You finally allow yourself to make one person proud… you are proud of you. You couldn't care less what or how they respond or anyone else. I am proud, acknowledge, and recognize myself. I am no longer looking to others for that sense of approval. No one has the power to tear me down or build me up but one person.

Me, myself, and I.

When you have healed, there will no longer be that emotional charge to their attacks on you. They will ignore, finger point, scoff, mock, or put out that hurtful "joke" on a flaw you used to hate about yourself, but now you're ready for it. You gauge all of your emotional reactions to their criticisms as an indicator of your negative inner voice. Whatever emotions come up, focus on acknowledging, releasing, and replacing with self-love, forgiveness, and compassion.

They will try to pull you into their head games at every opportunity. Do you remember how we talked about triggers? That means you have an over the top reactive emotional response to their attacks. Inspect what they are scoffing, mocking, or criticizing and check yourself. Is this something you criticize about yourself? See if the anger they display is a mirror to self-anger you have about yourself and whatever the XYZ quality is on the chopping block for the moment.

If they don't give you credit or scoff at your achievements, make sure you give yourself credit. Do not rely on others to develop your love and appreciation for what you do. Often a narcissist will scoff, mock, or make a disapproving look when you are shining in your talents and gifts. It's a key indicator. They feel like the "limelight" may be threatened.

Will their tactics work? Can they shape us out of our authentic self and gifts by making us feel uncomfortable?

Once you understand the dynamics, you see beyond their behavior and then allow it to show you the healing work you need to do. Suddenly when the narcissist talks negatively to you, there's this inner dialogue going on inspecting yourself to see, "Is this my negative inner voice, insecurities, and fears?" If they say something to intentionally hurt your feelings, ask yourself is there any guilt, shame, anger, etc. I have for myself and this quality. Or was I shining in my authentic self and inner light, so it triggered the disapproval of the narcissist? Have I allowed people to shape me out of who I truly am at my core to avoid criticism or make them feel comfortable?

#3 - Have you ever noticed the narcissist bending over backward for other people while they completely tear down your every request for any help what-so-ever? In a business relationship, you will have contracted for services with them. There is an exchange here where you pay for something they offer. Yet, when you request those services, they make you feel bad for asking about details, delivery terms, or following through on their end of the bargain. In friendships or other family ties, they create these same feelings.

What's going on here? During the love-bombing, they treated you like the most fantastic person on Earth. What's happening now? Everything in life revolves around their goals, needs, and desires. You are not even on the list anymore. Someone or something else is, and they are throwing it in your face. Your goals, needs, and desires are never recognized or minimized. Yet, we do this same thing to ourselves.

We put everyone else first. It's not healthy to not include yourself on your priority list. Yet, we do it. The self-sacrificing personality type creates suffering. Here we have met up with the narcissist to painfully mirror how we treat ourselves, back to us.

I AM NOT A PRIORITY attracts
YOU ARE NOT A PRIORITY.

These feelings can be a carry-over from childhood. Every time the child asks the parent to do, give something of themselves or have to focus on them, it creates hostility in the parent. You and your needs can not bother them. Suddenly, they are too busy. There are so many pressures on them. Here you are adding to the list of stress. Shame on you! You should be there for them without wanting, needing, or asking for anything.

As an Empath this creates a very traumatic experience because we are creating some stress for everyone. Being who we are means having questions, worries, fears, and needs. To not create waves, we take what appears to be the easier route. We let go of our own needs, wants, desires, and take the one person off of the priority list that we can. Ourselves. Our needs are scoffed, minimized, and pushed aside as irrelevant and inconvenient.

The narcissist has brainwashed us with their techniques to make us feel like we are the ones being needy and demanding. They have disapproving looks, comments, and hostility when we need them to show up for us. Avoiding the negativity means shrinking and minimizing ourselves. It looks like an easier path, but it's not.

Our inner issues create the narcissists playground.

That way, the narcissist does not have to be accountable. They do not have to uphold their part of the relationship, business deal, friendship, or parental obligations. At the heart of you are these real, valid issues. They need to be faced and addressed. The external patterns with people continually reinforce the unhealed internal trauma. The narcissist is just handing us the situations to reinforce the imbalance inside of us.

We don't fight, feel, or believe that we should be a priority.

You will even see the narcissist making other people the priority and throwing it in your face! We will call these little pawns the "triangle person." With a narcissistic parent or some family relationship, one child becomes "the favorite." That child is showered with love and attention while the other child is de-valued and discarded. All the golden child's imperfections are overlooked while they hammer the other child for everything they do.

Even if they do a million amazing things right, that will not matter. The narcissist will not see it or acknowledge them. These "triangles" are another tool in the mind manipulation toolbox that narcissists love to use. On purpose, they make comments as to exactly how they are favoring and prioritizing the "triangle person." They want it to be prominent and painfully known that you are not valid or loved in the same way. It must be you. They adore and bend over backward for this other person.

If your boss or career dynamics are trapping you with a narcissist, you will find the boss has a "pet" person. You will slave away for them while this incompetent person will get all the attention, perks, and promotions. The unhealed Empath is working away diligently to see someone else get the support and admiration. Yet the pain and suffering stems from seeing the situation from the unhealed standpoint.

The treatment matches the inner wounds we carry.

The healthy version of ourselves makes us a priority in balance with others. We will fight for ourselves. If no one makes us a priority, it doesn't matter because we make ourselves a priority. If we do not feel heard, we listen to our inner voice. If they do not honor us, we honor ourselves. When people in our circles do not treat us the way we treat ourselves, we walk away or no longer engage in the relationship. No one has the power over our self-esteem, approval, or value.

Once we do these things for ourselves, then and only then can we attract the job, relationship, or life situation that makes us a priority. If we can come to terms and admit all these core issues, we can heal. They are behaving as they should be, so we finally address this issue and heal. If you want out of the suffering, you've got to work on yourself.

Make yourself a priority. Step up to the plate and start setting boundaries for your wants, needs, dreams, and goals. Create healthy triangles with people who love and support you. Watch the narcissistic head games with a new set of eyes. If emotionally, it makes us feel unloved, insecure, or personal low worth, we do the inner work to flip the switch. We no longer give anyone else power to define us.

All crazy-making tactics are here to show, develop, and strengthen us. We hit that inner strength where we make ourselves a priority and fight for us even when no one else does. No matter what anyone thinks, I have a valid contribution here. I am worth taking the time to have my questions and concerns answered. I deserve the time and energy necessary to have my issues voiced and addressed. I am valid, and so are my feelings. I deserve to be adored and loved with not only words but actions.

Setting boundaries, standing for yourself as a priority, and becoming balanced in this area will not be easy. Get comfortable with making others uncomfortable. When they roll out the red-carpet head games, you'll have to keep standing up for yourself. Several tactics may be used against you. They may even twist things to make them look like the victim!! You will have to overcome many elements to become a balanced partner. They are not used to this and will not like the evolved version of you.

However, we can and need to take action for us. How can we expect anyone else to if we won't do it for ourselves? We need to open our eyes, hearts, and souls. Our internal weak spots are being hit over and over. We realize we could never voice our concerns, needs, worries, or fears and see them as valid. We invalidate, muffle our own needs, and make everyone else a priority first. The relationship is our mirror. They are just upholding their end of the bargain by invalidating, dishonoring, and not prioritizing us.

We need the painful part of the relationship to show us what is already inside of us.

We must face this element within ourselves. Then do the personal work in our lives and within our relationships to stand for the one person we always put on the back-burner. Ourselves. We are the person who we do not feel has valid concerns, fears, questions, or needs. We need to voice them and stand for ourselves with compassion for others. We need to decidc we deserve to be loved with time, attention, and energy. Not only when we fit "their" agenda.

#4 - Empaths sit on the fence in a beautiful land where making decisions is harder for them. We are a barrage of thoughts about every move we make. We think about the ripple effect of how everything affects every person we touch. We are entirely in tune with others to the point if we have to do something that will hurt someone else's feelings, we agonize and over-analyze. Narcissists have no problem making decisions because they only think or consider themselves and what they want. Now, this looks like a comfortable space for the Empath to hide because the narcissist will gladly take over your decision making for you.

HIGHLY SENSITIVE and INDECISIVE
attracts INSENSITIVE and DECISIVE

The narcissist can decide everything, and we don't have to be accountable. They are a stronger personality, and we are the weaker reflection. We lean and depend on their decisions. It means we don't have to think about all this information coming through our senses. They want to take over, and we want them to until we see they have no concern, empathy, or genuine care for us or others. All of their decisions revolve around what fits the narcissist's needs.

Until we decide we want to heal this part of ourselves, we will continue to put ourselves in this wheel because it fits! We enjoy letting someone else make the decisions and thinking for us. It appears easier. We are the ones that say let me see what my spouse, friend, boss, neighbor, etc. thinks when faced with a decision? Then we hash it around over and over on what to do?!?! Handing over our power to them looks so much easier. BUT, in the long run, it creates our suffering because narcissists are terrible decision-makers. They only care about themselves, and if we are happy it makes them unhappy. They like to see other's pain!

Unless we get back in the driver seat and make healthy decisions in our lives, we will be caught in this dysfunctional dynamic. We are letting someone run our life who would sabotage our happiness on purpose. How is that going to work out for us? Terribly. We need to get into our bodies, start facing the world, and make decisions again. They are forcing us to grow up and out of a very long parent-child dynamic. Plus, they are confrontational, and like control, so they won't turn things over to you quickly.

Once again, if narcissists weren't designed this way, we would never have to find a balance. We could hide behind them forever because they would be a genuine, safe space. Yet, we would never grow into our true potential and the highest versions of ourselves. Life is waiting for every single one of us to become all we are capable of being, doing, achieving, and fulfilling. Get back into the driver seat. You will be amazed at how much better the evolved you is at being behind the wheel.

#5 - I know. I know. You wanted a book where we can blame the toxic people and point the finger, but those days are over. All that is happening here is the soul mate, friend, boss, or relationship shows up painfully pointing out unresolved inner issues. Most of us have heard the saying, "Kids should be seen and not heard." What happens as those kids grow up?

I DO NOT DESERVE TO BE HEARD attracts

I AM THE ONLY ONE THAT DESERVES TO BE HEARD

Whatever your opinion or feelings are, they will be minimized. Your life and responsibilities are not nearly what the narcissist is currently handling. Your job is much easier. You don't understand their needs. Your input on decisions is not considered. They will belittle you if voiced. The Empath's thoughts and feelings are completely disregarded.

It's like screaming for help while you're drowning. The narcissist is looking at you gasping for air, hands waving, and your mouth barely above water. They coldly say, "You're not drowning." Then, walk away.

Here is a note on how we as parents can also help our children healing with the narcissistic relationship. Now I am in marriage number two with the covert narcissist. Our daughter got stung by a scorpion twice. The narcissistic dad disqualifies her experience. He tells her, "You didn't get stung. That didn't hurt you." Scorpion bites are terribly painful.

Yes, yes, she did get bit and it does hurt. She has to recognize her feelings, trauma, and pain, regardless of anyone else. I validated her feelings. The narcissist did not, but she painfully connected to the narcissist. Why doesn't he care about me? The outer treatment of her was attempting to show her the emotional issue. If she does not learn how to recognize, validate herself, or clearly see her experience, the soul wound continues. She may grow up physically and move away but emotionally, the new messenger will show up. This is precisely how the mirrors and laws of attraction work.

I openly talked about the scorpion bite with my daughter. We discussed how important it is to validate yourself, your experiences, opinions, and pain even when others won't. The healing pattern can now replicate. We can help our children. I firmly believe the narcissistic parent is the first chance to heal. Yet, if as parents, we are unhealed, we have no idea how to show them what inner work should be done.

Don't give anyone else the power to dictate what you think, feel, or believe. Make your feelings, thoughts, and ideas a priority. If my daughter can work out this issue with her dad, she will know the keys to healing and not get hooked into the cycle of suffering. These scenarios repeat if she does not understand its purpose or do the inner work.

If you find yourself in these positions where "they don't listen to me" it's just an experience to reflect. You internally feel your opinion isn't valid. Your thoughts are not deserving of consideration. You should be seen but not heard. Besides, a narcissist knows we won't fight for ourselves. So, tell me if you won't fight for yourself, how do you expect to attract people who will?

Start doing the inner work here by speaking up and acknowledging yourself. No one can do that for you. "I deserve to be heard. I have a valid opinion. My thoughts and experiences are valuable." Regardless of what anyone else does or thinks, you need to honor your voice, feelings, pain, and experiences. Until you get that place in your soul development, you will continue to attract relationships, work situations, and life placements that mirror this inner crack in your soul.

#6 - This isn't about changing the narcissist. I hope that is clear. Narcissistic relationships are about the inner work we need to do. Make yourself a priority. Stop being available for the narcissist's whims. Don't let them walk all over you. When they say jump, stop asking, "how high?" We are the ones who attracted this relationship by these imbalances.

CAN'T SET BOUNDARIES attracts
OVERSTEPS YOUR BOUNDARIES

The people-pleaser will want to scream if we have to say no to anyone. We will sacrifice ourselves to save any kind of criticism, judgment, or lack of approval from people. I will be there. I can help you with that. I can't say no to anyone. Awe, we are so much fun as our own personal worst enemy, much less thinking about the narcissists.

Think about the things you complain about and ask yourself some questions. Have I created this by my people-pleasing, inability to say no, or set boundaries for myself? Listen to the things you complain about and then think well, did I tell them no? Did I create this by taking on more than I can accomplish? If you have trouble doing any of those things, all the perfect situations will come into your life to remind you. People will take complete advantage of you. Plus, they will have no skill set to look deeper into the situation to see they are out of line and being inconsiderate with what they are asking of you.

Oh, you have 200 projects that need to be done by Friday, and the office narcissist asks, "Can you do this one for me too?" They only have five projects on their list. Here you are spinning in frustration, anger, and buried under your mountain of work when they stop by to let you know they have to take a couple of hours off to watch their kid's baseball game. You have worked late every night and missed your kid's games. Are you pissed yet? Did you rant and rave about them and victimize yourself when it's your inner imbalance that keeps showing up?

Learn to say no, kill the inner people pleaser, ask for help, and stop letting the egomaniac that "can do it all" run your show.

Once you set some of your boundaries, they will wonder what happened to their puppet?!? You will have to stand your ground, and most likely, that involves stepping over fear. If it's a boss, you may lose your job, your spouse may walk away from you, or your family member may disown you. That's how narcissists create spiritual tests. What will you choose living in fear or having faith?

There's usually some way these people are connected to us where we feel trapped in the situation. They control the finances, children, housing, or some dynamic where we think they "own us." We will have to step through that fear and honor ourselves. Otherwise, this would be easy. Learning to balance your scales here will be the best thing you have ever done. Start small if you need to with little things and work your way into those more significant steps. Learn to say no to others when they are crossing the lines expecting unrealistic ideals or using you. Stop orchestrating your band playing games of self-inflicted suffering!

You will have to get STRONG in defining what are my needs? Maybe its college classes, but you have kids at home. The narcissist can't be pinned down to help. Or when you need to study, they will sit on the couch oblivious to helping with the kids. You can't get anything done because "Mom I need… mom she hit me… mom, I'm hungry," stands in the way.

All the while, the narcissist is zoned into a movie or their phone unhelpful to YOU. You will have to get over yourself. Stand up for your needs and make the narcissist accountable. Even if they do not become helpful, you are conquering a colossal mountain. You are setting boundaries without fear of the narcissist.

Only in this relationship with someone so obviously taking ALL the time, energy, and resources for their needs would you develop an inner strength. A healthy person would respect your boundaries. They would push you to your personal best. We can only attract those personality types once we become that for ourselves.

#7 – Have you ever heard the song "Sweet Dreams" by the Eurythmics?

> *"Sweet dreams are made of this*
> *Who am I to disagree?*
> *I travel the world and the seven seas,*
> *Everybody's looking for something.*
>
> *Some of them want to use you*
> *Some of them want to get used by you*
> *Some of them want to abuse you*
> *Some of them want to be abused by you."*

This song hits on a critical universal truth and communicates how relationships are merely reflections. Givers attract takers. If you are ashamed of yourself, you will meet someone who shames you. If you feel guilt or low self-worth about some element of yourself, you find that counter match to hammer it home with their comments, criticisms, and behaviors. And so, the wheels of relationship dynamics make these locking connections holding people together.

Those people who find themselves in narcissistic relationships almost always find they have a hard time receiving. Empaths feel unworthy of love, money, success, and all the treasures the world has to offer. They give up their fair share of the pie so someone else can have more. Narcissists believe the world should show up for them on a platter, and so it does. We bargain shop while they are buying eccentric toys. Also, they only give to keep the scorecard going, twist, and inflate their contribution, and then use it to receive more than their fair share.

Everything they do has a hidden agenda. You want to be honest with yourself here and see what's reflecting. How difficult is it for me to receive? Do you buy things for everyone else, but for yourself, you cannot validate spending the money? Do you feel awkward when someone does something for you? You consciously make sure you give something back? Otherwise, you feel guilty.

If you have something you want, will the narcissist undermine your needs? Is there always money for them. When it comes to you, "money is tight, let's wait" shows up or "you don't really need that." Yet, whatever they need, they rationalize, however eccentric as necessary. They have a million reasons they think what they need is valid, and what you need is not important.

Narcissists have a constant scorecard going on in their minds. The scorecard is jaded in their direction. They do not live in reality. This tit for tat mentality is their ruler. They validate everything they give by an exchange happening in their direction. There is always an ulterior motive for what they offer. ALWAYS!

As liars and manipulators, they will make you feel like you get and have everything. Yet, if you start spending money on yourself, they will make you feel guilty or ashamed. You bought something for you, and so the comments, scoffs, or their disapproval of you becomes known. Start asking yourself some self-reflection questions.

Is this a match for me? I feel guilty or ashamed if I spend money on myself. If someone does something for me, I have to do something for them. If you have a hard time receiving their comments, bad looks, or confrontations will affect you emotionally, mentally, and spiritually. This extends to anything you do, not just money.

ASHAMED attracts YOU SHOULD FEEL ASHAMED

GUILTY attracts YOU SHOULD FEEL GUILTY

CANNOT RECEIVE attracts CANNOT GIVE

Narcissists are bloodhounds for anywhere you may have guilt or shame inside of you. Start looking at your conversations with a new set of eyeballs. Listen, feel, and find out when, how, and about what gets you going, razzled, or frazzled. What stories keep rolling around and around in your head?

We can use every time we emotionally react to them and feel ashamed, guilty, or wounded as a personal barometer pinpointing where we need to heal. No one can make us feel ashamed or guilty unless we already have guilt or shame inside of us. Every time you feel "bad" and you think it's generated by them switch your perspective. Is this matching an internal trauma? Is their criticizing tactics matching your inner voice to yourself? They are just vocalizing how you are beating yourself up so you can see it and finally address the internal weakness.

When you understand the core of the human design, you find that where this finger-pointing is happening is a mirror image wound. The narcissist themselves have repressed guilt, shame, feelings of low self-worth, etc. and instead of knowing how to see, acknowledge, and heal them, they try to pass them off on you.

You can look at those internal issues that are being picked apart and blown out of proportion by the narcissist right in the eye. Maybe you're an emotional-eater, and here the narcissist is mocking how much food is on your plate. Perhaps you lay on the couch all day and feel lazy to get reprimanded by the narcissist when they get home. "You're so lazy." The self-hate and guilt they are triggering is already inside you. We could go on with a hundred examples of this.

There's some internal soul clean up that can be done easily once you realize what is happening. Next time they criticize, shame, guilt, or finger point see if it matches where you shame, guilt, blame, and criticize yourself. Monitor yourself just as much as you monitor everyone else. If you feel guilty or ashamed of yourself in any way, the soul mate relationship will show up to hammer you on it. Until you choose unconditional self-love over conditional love and self-anger, the soul mates attract. We will get more into the actual healing tactics in another chapter. Still, we must know how to identify the inner wounds. The universe must bring the narcissist or you will never address the core wounds.

"For most people, their spiritual teacher is their suffering. Because eventually the suffering brings about awakening." Eckhart Tolle

#8 - Narcissists are negative and critical of everything and everyone naturally. Covert narcissists do not appear this way during the love-bombing. Yet as time wears on, it starts to bear its ugly face. Now, why would you as an Empath attract someone that's continuously a negative vibe? Empaths are happy and loving, mostly about people and life. You get involved with keeping the partner, friend, co-worker, etc. propped up all the time. Interestingly enough, you have to talk them into having fun, going places, and doing things with you. It makes no sense to us!

When you put a compassionate person who is a sponge for other people's emotions in with a naturally negative person, what happens? DRAIN CITY! Part of our spiritual purpose here is sealing off ourselves from negative forces. We are meant to live in a constant state of positive emotions. The negativity when you do not know how to seal off your energy field or emotional self will wipe you out.

You will get affected by their attitude, pulled into the negative wheel. Healing here means not letting anyone in your bubble. Constantly staying in a positive state of emotions regardless of the storms that narcissists create is the official mission. Especially since we have our heart involved in everyone being happy. We have to let go and realize that some people will always be negative and unhappy. Allow them to have their journey, but don't let them ruin yours.

POSITIVE VIBE attracts NEGATIVE VIBE

#9 - Anytime you move out of their idea of who you should be, the narcissist will trigger another inner wound: abandonment and betrayal. The narcissist will threaten to replace, leave, or kick you out at a moment's notice of our independence in arguments and disagreements. If it's a job, having your opinions and standing behind them may mean getting fired. You are not acting in a manner that supports their illusion. Or if you've formed your idea and go against their "superior knowledge" this threatens their false sense of self. They feel threatened, and they reject anyone who does not fit into their grand illusion. You don't serve a purpose to them anymore.

The tactic keeps us walking on eggshells and giving in to their demands. Truthfully though at a soul level, we abandoned and betrayed ourselves when we entered a toxic relationship. We didn't trust our gut instincts.

There are always signs and ways we may know we are right, but we don't voice our own opinions. We betray ourselves to go with the flow. We don't want to ruffle the narcissist's feathers. Instead of being our true authentic selves, we have become what they wanted us to be. We sold ourselves out, becoming molded and shaped into a tool.

ABANDON AND BETRAY attracts SELF-ABANDONED AND SELF-BETRAYED

Our souls desperately want us to become that solid sense of support, love, and acknowledgment that stands behind us. We have set up everyone to abandon and betray us until we get to that inner solidity. I will never abandon and betray myself. When no one is here for me, I am here for myself. When no one has my side, I have my side. When no one hears my cries, I hear my cries. You need to be solid and unwavering in yourself.

Take all the appropriate actions to love, honor, and care for you. Then you will be able to attract a partner, career, or life situation that mirror self-love rather than self-abandonment and betrayal. If you don't feel supported, honored, and loved, you do not have that inner relationship.

#10 – Have you figured out the narcissist is trying to sabotage you? You have partnered with someone incapable of being supportive or having a co-sharing relationship where both parties contribute and want the best for one another. In their underhanded covert ways or flat out front and center attacks, they want to tear you down. It's like trying to do a set of push-ups with someone sitting on you. Maybe it's a hobby or passion you love, and every time you take the time for yourself, they pitch a fit. Maybe you just quit smoking to have them blow smoke right in your face. Maybe you start an exercise plan but can't make it to the gym because of some drama or emergency, and they "need you."

SABOTAGE YOU MEETS SABOTAGE OURSELVES

You ultimately will be stronger after this once you get through all the self-development. No one can sabotage our fun unless we allow it. We are weak to their tactics and techniques because of our imbalances and inner unhealed wounds. Once you breakthrough, they cannot touch you.

You make time for yourself and friends without getting distracted by their displays of drama. You plan to go to the gym and stick to it. You quit smoking and follow through even though they left that pack of cigarettes in your car staring at you. That cake they brought over because they forgot you're on a diet, say no. I don't want a piece. I'm on a diet.

Go ahead, make plans with your friends. Do not let anyone stand in your way of going on enjoying life. Join a club, reconnect with old friends, and allow yourself people and activities outside of the narcissist. Co-dependent becomes independent. Set boundaries and stand for them. Plan trips and do not get absorbed in the narcissist tactics to become the complete center of attention. Stop withdrawing into yourself and away from friendships regardless of how it affects the narcissist. Don't walk on eggshells or get intimidated by their temper tantrums. Realize that you are running your show and get accountable.

Our attractions with one another are all being broadcast out by these different components. Our bodies are made of these magnetic charges, all working together to create invisible bonds. We don't understand these concepts, so it becomes frustrating. How or why do we keep getting into similar situations with people? These become "repeat patterns" for us. If we stay in the blame and finger-pointing game, we stay stuck.

If we look at the situation as a teacher, we can truly evolve.

These concepts are critical in healing. Otherwise, when that wonderful person comes into your life that treats you like the Queen Bee or King of the Earth, you will push them away. I know it sounds brain-boggling. Why would we not be attracted to a healthy partner? Because we have not become a healthy partner to ourselves. We may not want to admit it, but it's the truth. Until they teach us what we need to know, we will walk away from the most beautiful people and straight into the arms of someone "toxic".

These invisible energetic cords lock us into the perfect dynamics.

If you changed your perspective as we've been discussing and drew out on a piece of paper, every toxic relationship, what would it look like? How do they make you feel? Use how everyone treats you to self-assess

YOU, not them. Think about the mirrors we have discussed. Rather than complaining about them, ask yourself, what is my internal trauma that attracted this person? What action steps do I need to take to heal?

I know the pain of narcissistic relationships, and I want us all to do the personal work to break free of these invisible prisons. That can only truly happen when we transform ourselves out of our unhealthy patterns. We have to take charge and be responsible as our own healer.

CHAPTER 5

TRAUMA TRIBULATIONS

DO YOU REALIZE you are getting a completely different explanation of why the narcissist is precisely the way they need to be? Even the famous loop of "love-bombing, discard, and de-value" is a strategic character element to promote our growth. The narcissist is telepathically engineered to know the exact combination of adoration and abuse to keep you hooked into the relationship. We know something is wrong, but we don't know exactly what?!?

Covert narcissists can be so charming and loving professing their idolization of us to everyone. Yet, in private, they completely ignore, criticize, and manipulate us. One moment they show up attentively taking care of us in the most amazing ways. Ten minutes later, they are giving us the riot act about some small request. Let's take the confusion out of this and get to the heart of your matching inner wounds.

They have these personality traits so we will not walk away from our relationship with them. The keys to the trauma we carry within come to the surface in these relationships. Narcissists are the most potent key in relaying our inner trauma back to us. We have a mission. Decode the relationship situations, heal the emotional trauma, and your broken parts.

Which once we get clearly defined on this tango of pain, you will completely understand how to re-wire your responses by healing. Once you can accomplish this mission, the "chemical loop" addiction to abuse will vanish. The energetic cords that connect you will no longer be a match. Everything in the body is designed mentally, emotionally, and energetically to lock us with the narcissist until we do the self-work.

We have touched on this briefly, but decoding this cycle is vital in healing. The narcissist sets the bait. The wounded soul is swimming in their love that seals the internal cracks. This beautiful, fantastic person has finally shown up to love you just as you are faults, weaknesses, insecurities, and imperfections. In a sense, our ego's our basking in their limelight, and we love the attention.

They are genuinely filling up your empty holes and putting you first in all ways. It creates the illusion of how wonderful you are and what a great relationship this will be. The narcissist's intense focus on being the dream situation, job, partner, or relationship/life situation, is dazzling and dream-worthy. We want to believe it.

Narcissists have a divine ability to pull us in with their charm, promises, and this telepathic gift that knows what we want to hear. In relationships, the fairy tale kind of love draws us to them and wants so desperately to live in its illusion. In a career, it seems like the "dream job." In friendship, it's that period when they appear interested in us, thoughtful, and helpful. They know exactly how to reel us into their web.

Whoever the narcissist dropped and de-valued to make you the high priority is hurt. You may not even know who these other people are if you've just come into the narcissists trap, but be sure they are there. They remember how wonderful the "love-bombing" felt as the narcissist puts them into discard and de-value to shower you with love and attention. All the people on the narcissist list become key in creating these perfect dynamics, the narcissist being the center focus of lots of attention and energy.

That's when we fall into the trap and believe the illusion they create. Our hearts are involved, and we have given them our trust, admiration, and confidence. We give ourselves wholly and entirely to them. Now you are cornered into the next phase that opens you painfully up to your internal soul cracks. That's when the discard phase unfolds so slowly that you never honestly know what or how anything wrong is happening.

At first, it may be some joking comments to make you feel insecure. Or you notice that once flamingly beautiful, considerate soul is now ignoring you completely. All the while, other people are now the shining objects of their attention. They will bend over backward for others while being rude, controlling, or simply ignoring you and your needs. Yet, now you're bending over backward for them because you have placed your trust and faith in the relationship dynamic. This switch from the idolizing or love-bombing to the de-value phase is so important.

In this idolize cycle, the narcissistic is getting energy from you by your admiration, trust, faith, belief in them, and their illusion. They adore you. You adore them. Think about it like the snake in the Garden of Eden. The snake is selling the apple and appealing to your ego. Look at all of the shiny things you will have if you put your faith in me. You took a bite.

Now, the show is over. Reality can show up. What you have trusted in was a lie you wanted to believe and fit all your broken parts. The head games, manipulations, and triangles with people can now begin. We don't understand the real purpose of this phase. It's just very confusing and hurtful. We don't intentionally try to hurt others.

We start questioning. Did they have no intention of keeping to their promises? Comments or secrets they've been holding come out. You've trusted and committed to them, but they have left you high and dry. You suddenly are not a priority at all. Someone or something else is now the object of their attention while they cast you aside painfully. We take this personally and don't understand their behaviors. Our minds reel in a new way about them, often wondering what we've done to lose our position in their admiration.

Why are they hurting me? Why would they do that? How can they be so cold, insensitive, and emotionally void of feelings suddenly? Why am I not enough? What did I do? We become wounded, and their rejection of us matches our internal rejection of us. They have essentially become the drug dealer of our love, support, approval, and admiration. Once they pull the plug on the "love-bombing," we are flailing like a fish out of water. Floundering around trying to be what they need so the drug dealing "love bomber" will come back.

We are so wounded inside. We do not understand how to be that provider of love and support to ourselves. This discard and de-value phase must create suffering for us, so we will finally learn how to be, do, and provide ourselves with love, approval, admiration, and support. That's where we will take this internal trauma in a new direction — healing instead of hurting. They are handing us the keys into the depths of our soul. We need to dissect, analyze, and allow the situations to strengthen us by changing our perspective. What exactly do we need to heal within, and how do we do this so-called self-work?

PHASE 1: Shower you with attention, gifts, and promises of the future!

This phase is the illusion the narcissist creates to pull you in, and as genuine people, we think this is authentic. We genuinely want a relationship with both parties, giving, loving, and partnering together.

Spiritual lesson: Identify how they control and pull you in by feeding your ego. They are the snake in the tree luring you in with treats, giving you attention, and soaking you in adoration. When we rely on others to provide us with our approval, love, support, and self-worth, it leaves us wide open. This is a space inside you that no one ever taught you how to be for yourself. Authentic, realistic self-love and approval is the only answer to breaking away from your co-dependency to this phase. You must become a solid sense of love and support to yourself no longer relying on outside sources, people, or situations. We also must learn how to recognize who to trust by consistent actions rather than promises, grand ideals, and illusions.

PHASE 2: Pull away from us no longer showing us kindness or appreciation. They cast us away like old news. The person who made us feel so loved, supported, and appreciated ignores us. Won't give us the time of day anymore. Won't answer our texts. The thoughtful comments become rude remarks or disapproving looks designed to hurt us. We don't understand that this is intentional, and we become deeply wounded. We feel used and betrayed as we realize we believed a bunch of empty promises.

Spiritual lesson: No matter who abandons or betrays us, we will never abandon and betray ourselves. We are our source of love and support un-wavered by the actions of others. We learn to dissect the exact things that are emotionally triggering us following the self-realization and mirrors chapters. Use this phase as a tool to map out your soul issues. Is where they criticize you where you internally criticize yourself? Are you co-dependent? Are you a people pleaser who can't set boundaries? You must tackle a new to-do list. You work on you. Focus all the time you used to put into them, into healing yourself. Once you have completed the mission, you will see the tactics used during this phase as a marker of your personal growth and development. You will only feel gratitude, unconditional love, and forgiveness as the narcissist becomes crucial in seeing those weaknesses and wounded parts.

PHASE 3: The narcissist, in the meantime, has made someone else their shiny prospect. We are left to watch them shower someone else with that same attention we once received. On purpose, they will push this in front of our faces. They are designed to show us these insecurities and make us feel jealous. As deep caring, sensitive individuals, we take this personal. We wonder what is wrong with us? Why don't they do those things for me anymore? We remember how wonderful it feels to be their shiny object of idolization.

Spiritual lesson: We are guilty of jealousy and envy, so we do not make judgments of others if they fall into the trap. Jealousy and envy are still inside of us, but we can transform the reaction to admiration. Insecurity is still inside of us, but we can turn that into confidence. Fear of abandonment and betrayal are inside of us. Nevertheless, we can move that into self-love and unwavering self-loyalty regardless of what anyone else does or does not do. We are no longer looking for our other half to give any of those things to us. We are not a half.

Friendships, partnerships, family members, and career situations may manifest in life differently than the example I used. However, the underlying tactic is still the same. Maybe the narcissist is bending over backward for their child or a family member while they won't do a single thing to help you. Perhaps the narcissistic friend is using another friend to create this triangle. This might be a business relationship or your boss. Mold your particular situation to fit those criteria and then apply the techniques to heal your soul.

Let's talk for a minute about jealousy, envy, and insecurity. Narcissists also supply us with massive spiritual tests above and beyond, showing us where we need to do soul work. They will lie, manipulate, and do whatever is necessary to get you to fall into these lower negative emotions. The loop created between these phases and the triangles between people they manipulate is the perfect set up.

At first, you are the one and only, most fantastic partner ever, and cherished completely. Next, you are just on a list of admirers lucky to have even gotten their attention. While they go out of their way for someone else, they are picking at every mistake you make and blowing it out of proportion to make you feel inadequate. Besides letting you know or think that you are easily replaceable.

These are crucial elements and personality qualities that you need to get stronger! Let's get into a real-life example of how this happens because sometimes these situations we do not see, much less know how to heal. When we are with partners who do not "cheat" on us in a physical relationship sense, it's not always easy to understand the small lower level games being played. If your narcissist does cheat, and you are aware they have issues with monogamy it's much easier to break down. You can use those situations in the same way as the examples.

I just want to really expand on situations that can be camouflaged in ways we may not see without an expert pointing them out.

Training time!

Case Study #4937:

Jim had been married to Mariah for 12 years when he came across the idea his lover and wife was a narcissist. Their relationship seemed to go through phases of ups and downs, like all married couples. She really could make him feel like the most wonderful man in the world. Not that she didn't know how to make him feel like pond scum too. But hey that's women… that's relationships… that's love… right? You know some of what she argued, nagged, and threw in his face well she was right.

He really loved her beauty, grace, and sense of humor. Other men admired her too. In a flash of that dazzling smile and wit, she could win anyone with her charm. She would make comments about other men flirting with her. He could replay a thousand ways she had told him about men gawking or complimenting her at work. Jim could even see the replay of the conversation in his mind sometimes.

"You know Jim that Marty guy was in with his wife today and said right in front of her. "your husband sure is a lucky man!" He always flirts with me even if she is with him. I joke and laugh, but I feel so embarrassed by the whole deal, you know. God, how does that make her feel? I know he thinks I'm sexy. She has to know it too."

(In a narcissist's mind everyone wants what they have, is impressed by them, or wishes they could be with them. They are very good at self-promotion and do not mind twisting situations, gaslighting, or manipulating others to reach the top. If we have the opposing imbalance, we are terrible at self-promotion even if we have amazing talents. We are the opposite reflection and make self-defeating commentary.)

Or this one the other day…

"I was out to lunch with the girls today, and guess what happened? The waiter dropped me his phone number. What a funny sense of humor he had I couldn't help but flirt with him a little. He was almost ten years younger than me. I just had to giggle and laugh about it! Feels good to know I still got it going on. Aren't you a lucky man?"

She always seemed to pause in their somewhere and gaze at him. (When a narcissist pauses and gazes, pay attention. They are looking to provoke an emotional and energetic extraction.) She was judging his reaction, seeing if that dagger had appropriately splayed in his chest. His last girlfriend had cheated on him and broke his heart. The wound seemed to be still hanging on. He never understood why Mariah would tell him those things knowing his past and how sensitive of an area it was for him.

She would not cheat on him. Jim felt really solid about that! It was just the idea that she was flirting with other men that hurt. He felt so jealous. He worked hard to keep up with her standards. The truth was, he walked on eggshells for that woman. Just always trying to bend and conform to her never-ending demands.

Every time they disagreed, if he confronted her about his feelings, she would blow up, make Jim feel insecure, or ignore his arguments. The fighting just wasn't worth it, so he stopped communicating his feelings. There was just that pain that showed up over and over with her comments.

He had never thought they were placed there on purpose. The whole fact she had been building herself up while tearing him down never occurred to him. Jim was learning though that parts of him were still unhealed. The new education of his world meant a new understanding.

Do you see how Mariah is getting feedback by making him JEALOUS and INSECURE? And from feeling like other men ENVY her husband's relationship with her. She's feeding off of that shift that happens in Jim as he feels his heart drop into the deep gaping wound. She gives him that idolization attention, pulls away, and then mentions how "other men" want her. What would happen if Jim saw the manipulations behind this tactic?

Mariah is also an insecure counterpart needing to get validation from other men. She's wanting to make sure that Jim keeps trying to please her. This tactic ensures her constant attention. If Jim thinks a million other men are standing in line, she can feed her ego plus trigger the insecurity inside of him. That way, he gives her more and treats her better. She has been manipulating him in these almost invisible ways for years.

Jim, however, has to have the matching inner wound for this tactic to work. What if he loved himself regardless of who she flirted with or how she got attention, admiration, and feeling adored? He started to wonder how much of this was Mariah inflating the truth. Narcissists will lie, twist, and manipulate situations to make us jealous. What if her little tactic didn't work? He became unshakeable in his love for himself regardless of what she did. There would be no way for her to get him to drop into feeling insecure or jealous.

When you break this down, there is no one left to judge, blame, or finger point. Mariah, as a narcissist, is continuously empty inside. She must look for attention from lots of people because she is insecure and feels inadequate. Narcissists can never get enough attention from everyone else no matter what you do. They need constant ego attention and validation from outside sources. We have also been empty, insecure, and feeling inadequate inside. Precisely why the love bombing or idolization phase appealed to us.

Now he looks for those occasions to heal himself. He still has inner parts that do NOT feel completely secure and valid. Jim fears being abandoned and, in a sense, that's what the narcissist is doing in these small little encounters. Mariah has stated that she was flirting with someone else. That moment of her ego getting inflated was more critical than Jim and his feelings. It's hurtful when you do not understand the purpose.

This is how soulmates are designed, and even the euphoric feelings of "love" must make us blind. God (or insert whoever you call God) is a brilliant creator. He knew that we would not just sign up to do self-work and have our inner wounds triggered without feeling like a soul mate was some beautiful fairy tale of Prince Charming and Cinderella. Not all relationships are indeed bound with these ties, either. We get a mix of experiences here on Earth with people. Some are supporting and loving. Some are hurtful, but it's all in the name of growing without breaking.

Now is the time of evolution to restructure the old thought paradigms about relationships.

Soul mates are fascinating key players in our unhealed wounds, imbalances, belief systems, karma, and spiritual tests. No one here gives or takes anything from us. They are all just reflecting different elements of ourselves back to us as messengers. In this way, you are looking to form a checklist to soul investigate all situations that create suffering.

Is this person mirroring my internal weakness? (I am insecure. I base my sense of love, approval, and support as coming from outside myself. I have not yet deeply self-partnered?)

Is this an element of myself I need to balance? (How do I respond to people flirting with me?)

Is this somewhere I lack compassion or have made judgments about others, and I need to fix, heal, and evolve my actions? (You don't understand how people become "weird" checking other people's phones or get "crazy" with jealousy. Then you fall in love with a narcissist. The head games and lies lead you to become "crazy" with suspicion.)

Is this somewhere I have failed a spiritual test? (The ego can get triggered into lots of emotions. Jealousy, envy, resentfulness, bitterness, can all start swirling. Funny, it's the same things the narcissist feels, and here we are guilty. It's critical to unconditional love and forgiveness to recognize how the narcissist has triggered you into narcissism. This is one element that is not being fully expanded upon in the current healing programs I have seen available, and it's crucial to breaking the bonds of attachment.)

At first, you will have to see when those comments, actions, and tactics by the narcissist come up to make you jealous and insecure. Recognize what is happening and bask yourself in UNCONDITIONAL LOVE. I love myself right here at this moment, feeling jealous and inadequate. Through each exhale, I am going to blow out these negative feelings I've been storing in my body for so long. Then imagine them turning into smoke and disappearing. With each inhale, I will ground myself right here, right now, in unconditional love.

Now we are left with deeply self-partnering. That means you are a source of love, support, and unwavering loyalty to yourself regardless of what anyone else does or does not do. No matter who betrays and abandons me, I will never abandon and betray myself. We are not basing our security, source of love and approval, or confidence on anyone else. The narcissist is just the exact personality you need to enlighten and test you as they pull you through these loops of idolize, discard, and de-value.

Step 2, the Empath who most likely is a people pleaser, may have people who flirt with them. This is always flattering, and our egos love the attention of being admired and adored. When someone flirts with you, how do you react? Do you try to play it off, so you don't hurt anyone else? You don't want anyone to feel rejected, so you try to deal with them "nicely." Does the attention feed your ego, so you entertain it? There are always energies between everyone. What if you had an attractive client become flirtatious and your company is depending on their contract? How would you act?

While you are in a situation like this, reverse the roles. Look at it as an outsider pretending you are your spouse and see how you would feel. It's easy to rationalize our actions, so it's essential to do these role reversals. Besides, its true Empaths will shuffle their feelings to avoid hurting anyone's feelings. We know the pain of rejection and don't want anyone to feel that way. Skirting around these issues seems more comfortable.

I realize that as the wounded counterpart, we are not making flirtatious contact, cheating, or playing head games with others like narcissists. Still, we have to know how to handle attention in a way that honors our partner. The next time someone flirts with you, recognize that how you respond ultimately will reflect in the partner you attract. Ask yourself if my partner was in this situation, what would the reaction be that would make me feel loved, honored, and adored?

There are always several elements at work in a single situation. Becoming unshakeable in your self-love, confidence, and inner security regardless of the narcissist's games is life-changing. Plus, you are learning to continually honor your partner, set boundaries with those who make advances upon you and move beyond being inconsiderate. You can be tested as they may have pushed you into the discard and de-value phase while someone else is getting their attention. Here comes someone else who is adoring, admiring, and flirting with you. Being trustworthy in who you are and what you stand for regardless of what others do takes integrity.

If the narcissist is remaining jealous and insecure, realize that they are "projecting." For this reason, narcissists are insanely jealous personality types, so your every encounter with others triggers their guilt. Guilt for the way they flirt, tease, and play head games with their list of admirers. If anyone gets emotionally overworked in their accusations of you, but you are not guilty, it's because they are doing it.

If you are truly not flirting back and handling attention from people who are attracted to you in an evolved way that honors your partner, there will be NO GUILT they can trigger you into feeling. You will recognize this is their issue they cannot see, and you will not emotionally get worked up by their attacks. If you are guilty of flirting or whatever they accuse you of you will be triggered because you are not taking the right actions and you have a conscious.

If you have isolated yourself from others because of their insecurities, jealousies, and disapproval of outside friendships it's time to re-connect with people. The narcissist wants to have you at their whim, when they need you, and on their terms. If you have your own life outside of them it's impossible for them to extract the energy they need. As unhealed empaths we are magnets for draining relationships and so we truly do trust and get hurt by the wrong people. Isolating ourselves seems like the easy way out. It's not, especially when it's with the narcissist. Once you get educated and balance yourself the right friendships will fall into place. You will also be much more intuitive about who to trust.

Another element of this, which it's amazing how many triggers can be hit in one seemingly small incident. What if you get into an argument about this issue? You have real valid details of their flirtatious behaviors and voice them. They will not want to see, acknowledge, or accept the evidence as accurate. Twisting details, lies, gaslighting, or one of their various tactics may be used to escape being accountable. Stand solid in yourself, your beliefs, and opinions regardless of their tactics.

Or the narcissist may own up to these things making comments and throw other admirers in your face either openly or covertly. Just looking to see how much they can trigger you into jealousy and insecurity. They love to shock you, take you off your guard, and be completely inconsistent with their commentary. At one moment they admit it's an issue. Another moment they completely deny all charges. Covert narcissists are truly fascinating.

Maybe it's a different karmic tie. Perhaps we have lacked compassion for others who become "crazy" with jealousy and insecurity. How can we understand until we are there in those shoes? None of us want to play an investigator into our partner. You are questioning where they are or what they are doing with whom. Now you have a new basis of understanding for others and the irrational behaviors it can trigger. You will connect to them without judgment.

Narcissists are skilled manipulators too. Be fully aware of how they will lie to feed into their systems. When you are a truthful person, you don't look for lies from other people. They are pathological liars, which means they have no guilt, remorse, or conscious about making stories. Everything and everyone is a tool, and twisting reality is no problem. This is another way we "project" our qualities on other people. If we don't lie and twist the truth, we don't see this in others. Narcissists are usually much better judges of character than we are for this exact reason.

"Projection" can be where we don't see our faults but identify them in others, but it can also be where we think others have the same qualities we do. In the case of empaths and narcissists, this a combination for disaster. What we are seeking to obtain is an accurate picture of ourselves and others. That way, we can do our personal work, which is about our soul wounds, unhealed issues, and egoic lies and illusions of reality. When you truly awaken to narcissists, you realize that they live in fantasy land. You do too even if it's for opposite reasons.

For example, let's take this same couple and break down how this happens.

Jim starts a friendship with a guy named Bruce. They have a lot of the same interests, and kids both involved in softball. Mariah is dropping off their daughter at practice one day and see's Bruce. Bruce is dressed up for an interview that day in a nice suit. He's already mentioned this to Jim.

When Mariah gets home, she gloats about how good Bruce looked today. She shimmers around the kitchen and comments, "I told him if he were my husband, I wouldn't let him out of the house. He looks so handsome today!" Jim understands how these wheels work and can see beyond her scheme. He doesn't fall into her game. He feels jealousy stirring inside of him but blows it out and replaces it with admiration. Then makes a comment that surprises Mariah.

"Yep, he's a great-looking guy."

Her tactic doesn't work. Jim can pinpoint the disappointment in her attitude when he doesn't get jealous! Ha! Now she's the only one dropping into frustration and Jim's high on admiration and confidence rather than jealousy and insecurity. Later that day, when he talks to Bruce about his job interview, he pops off a random comment, "Ya, Mariah said she was teasing you today about how good you looked. She said she told you if you were her husband, she wouldn't let you out of the house."

Guess what Bruce replies? "No, she never said a word."

Mariah was lying about the situation to make Jim jealous and split up a possible friendship between them. She knows he will be less likely to be friends if he feels uncomfortable with the fact his wife is eyeballing him when they hang out. Narcissists don't like you to have friends. They want to isolate you, so all your attention revolves around them… and let's add a little side note.

They want you available on their terms, when they need you and snap their fingers. I want to do something with you that makes me look good, serves my purpose, or feeds my ego. Covert narcissists, you would think adore their families. It's all about the show and how things look to other people. The rest of the time, when there are no ego props to be gained, you're mainly getting the silent treatment, put-downs, or de-value and discard.

They are slaves to their egos, but the unhealed version of us is a slave to our egos too. Besides, they like to know they have control, and you are their puppet. When I snap my fingers, you come running. When we are still wounded, we do run when they snap. We are like refugees stranded in the desert, begging for a drink of water. We've isolated ourselves from other healthy relationships, so no one else is showing up here. After being ignored, criticized, mocked, and scoffed, the narcissist has graced you with some attention, adoring acts of kindness, or acted genuinely interested in you.

You feed into this situation by your weaker inner trauma's being hit time and again. Healing yourself is the only way out of "the abuse loop." If Mariah were married to God himself, she would still need to try to get attention, validation, and self-love from everywhere she could. Lower level narcissists get this from flirtatious attention and ego feeding. Higher-level narcissists bury themselves in affairs and all kinds of complicated relationship messes.

To be locked into co-partnering with this personality type, we have to have these matching inner wounds. The outside world is set up to trigger us into seeing this inside trauma that needs to heal. That is the land of soul revelation we are searching through this experience in a physical body on Earth. The TV show called your life is bringing back to you all these experiences.

The narcissistic qualities are necessary, vital, and critical components of this process. Once you become a solid sense of love, approval, and support of yourself regardless of the actions of others, you will break the cycle. The interlocking forces will bring you true loving, supporting relationships. All your insecurities, weaknesses, failed spiritual tests, and karma must be resolved. That is the only real way to end the dynamic between you and narcissists.

Narcissistic supply is about you, not them.

CHAPTER 6

THE KEYS OF NARCISSISTIC SUPPLY

WOULD YOU LIKE to get to the heart of narcissistic supply finally? Could people be connected to our spirits, draining us of our energy? Are there energetic cords connecting us all? Do energy vampires exist? The theories around narcissistic supply seem very well supported. We can and often do feel exhausted when we have experiences with certain people.

Let's see if I can break this down simply although the design concept is nothing other than miraculously spectacular in developing us. We are all nothing more than light being reflected at specific wavelengths to create this universe. Science is concurring the world we live in is a hologram. Some of you reading this may already have been introduced to this concept if not put "holographic universe" in your google search bar. What we see is a similar rendition of a reality show. TV Channel Earth. Science is catching up now and you can find all kinds of information on "the matrix".

What is in this invisible world of energy is a lot of coded soul information. We get into this more intensively in the last chapter, but for now, let's unravel this mystery of narcissistic supply. Narcissistic supply is nothing more than living in ego and our subconscious wounds that are still looking for love, approval, and support from outside ourselves. The unhealed

Empath has this same inner wounding. The reason we fell into the charms, manipulations, and love-bombing is because our egos are being fed. In essence, we are extracting narcissistic supply from them.

Look the perfect partner has shown up to love, approve, and elevate me. Isn't that what the narcissist is looking for too? At the heart of both parties are wounded people who decided to reject themselves at their core. They create the façade, and it is amazing. Yet, as all people looking to bury their issues in someone else the rug must be pulled out. Otherwise, none of us would want to heal.

It is my hopes that narcissists too will be able to do this same inner work. Once the unhealed Empaths stop feeding them energy it maybe their only choice. Until then both good and evil are a necessary part of the design plan. Living in ego creates suffering, no matter who you are and that is the heart of narcissistic supply. All of these variations are necessary for us to grow, expand, develop, and move through our fears, weak places, anxieties, failed spiritual tests, karma, and trauma. The situations, games, soul mates, and life patterns develop based on that soul information.

Look at the chart below and think of yourself and the people you are entangled with so you can do some assessments. What percentage am I operating off of here?

EGO	SPIRIT
ME	WE
Separation	Unity
Blame	Understanding
Hostility	Friendliness
Resentment	Forgiveness
Pride	Love
Complain	Gratefulness
Jealousy	Co-Happiness
Anger	Love
Power	Humble

Materialism	Spiritualism
War	Peace
Past/Future Orientated	Now Orientated
Coldness	Sympathy
Self-Denial	Self-Love
Living Up To This Or That	Just Be

Narcissists live in ego/false self a majority of the time. Think about your narcissist while you scroll through the list. How often have they pushed you to join them? There's a favorite proverb that the Indians would tell their young I have always loved and expands on this concept!

"There is a battle of two wolves inside us all. One is evil. It is anger, jealousy, greed, resentment, lies, inferiority, and ego. The other is good. It is joy, peace, love, hope, humility, kindness, empathy, and truth.

Who is the wolf that wins? The one you feed."

All of us have the white and black wolf inside of us. They are according to this chart, Buddha nature/true-self versus ego/false-self. Every single one of us on this planet is guilty of operating in darkness or ego. The only difference between people and their energetic beings is the amount of time or devotion we have in doing the personal work to remain in a constant state of light. The dark force is pushing on us every day in a million ways to WIN!

When you fall into ego or the false-self, you feed narcissistic supply.

The narcissist is designed on purpose to continually feed that black wolf (ego/false self) and trying to talk all the white wolves (Buddha nature/true self) into doing the same. When we have matching wounds, narcissistic supply gets triggered. For example, you are a people pleaser and cannot say no to others. Here is the narcissist who openly uses you and then leaves you high and dry. You drop into resentment, bitterness, and hate. Yet, when you start doing soul work, you realize it's those imbalances…

Cannot set boundaries pushes your boundaries.

Must be a commodity to be loved meets loves you for being a commodity.

Have not self-partnered meets the person who abandons and betrays you.

These situations would have created LOTS of negative emotions before. We would want to blame the narcissist and point our energy at them. Now we are getting to the heart of the situation, being accountable, and doing the self-work. The energy is directed at ourselves, healing, and stepping into our authentic truth.

You are setting boundaries.

The people-pleasing disaster within has healed. We can say no when needed because no one outside of us is in charge of our love and approval.

We finally decide to self-partner. No matter who abandons and betrays us, we will never abandon and betray ourselves.

We have re-entered life, made healthy triangles with people, and no longer codependently rely on them.

We could outline every element we discussed in the Self-Realization and Mirrors chapters to pinpoint how our imbalance is at the heart of the narcissistic supply.

Let's say you have a hard time voicing your opinions, feelings, and standing up for yourself. You expect people to be considerate of you without having to say anything or express your needs. The narcissist comes along with that insensitivity and self-centered tunnel vision. You've partnered with them in some way. They are making decisions that affect you but have no concern for you what-so-ever. The negative emotions start rolling around and around all about them. But if you stood your ground, voiced your concerns, and set boundaries, there would be no issues between you and them.

Maybe it's a way you failed a spiritual test that's holding you in the pattern. The narcissist at work just got a job promotion. Here you are the loyal, hard-working, excellent employee still slaving away while this newly graduated young punk just got your dream job. Will you hit jealousy and envy or admiration for them? Maybe that young punk is good at highlighting what he contributes and brings to the table. He runs around blowing up every small thing he does for the company. You quietly work away, expecting them to notice you. Certainly, they will see your value without saying anything. Lots of elements can be at work where we drop into lower emotions. We think it's about them, but it's about us.

The negative emotions and suffering are a brilliant delivery method. We can get over blaming them and victimizing ourselves. Start being accountable, doing the personal work, and moving out of these patterns. Stop feeding the beasts!

Scientifically speaking, there is a compelling body of work conducted by Dr. Emoto that beautifully supports how our thoughts affect our physical world. He consciously directed feelings like anger, love, and different emotions on samples of water. They froze the water to see if there were any differences in the molecular structure. The pictures and research results showing their effects on the molecular structure are amazing.

On the next page, you will find a sample of this work. You can check out more of Dr. Masaru Emoto's research online or in his book "The Hidden Messages of Water." As you look at the photographs of the structures, think about Buddha's most famous sayings. "Holding onto anger is like grasping a hot coal with the intent of throwing it at someone else; you are the one who gets burned. You will not be punished for your anger, you will be punished by your anger. You are the victim of your own anger." The concepts that spiritualists have been talking about since the beginning of time match the research.

Here are a few pictures to outline what I am talking about:

Here are some images of water crystals from Doctor Emoto's experiments, extracted from his website. More examples and more information about his work can be found at www.masaru-emoto.net/english/water-crystal.html.
MUSIC
Edelwise
A Heavy Metal Song
Amazing Grace
PRAYER
Water from the Fujiwara Dam BEFORE Buddhist prayer was offered.
The same water from the Fujiwara Dam AFTER Buddhist prayer was offered.
WORDS
"Eternal"
"You Disgust Me"
"Love and Gratitude"
"Thank You"
"Evil"

You can find many more on his website and so much more additional information at: http://www.masaru-emoto.net/english/index.html

What conclusions could we reach from thinking about positive and negative thoughts versus narcissistic supply? Are we changing our molecular structure constantly? Look at "You Disgust Me" in the bottom middle row. Has the narcissist ever made you feel literally sick?

Let's go a step further and see what does a healthy cell looks like compared to a cancer cell?

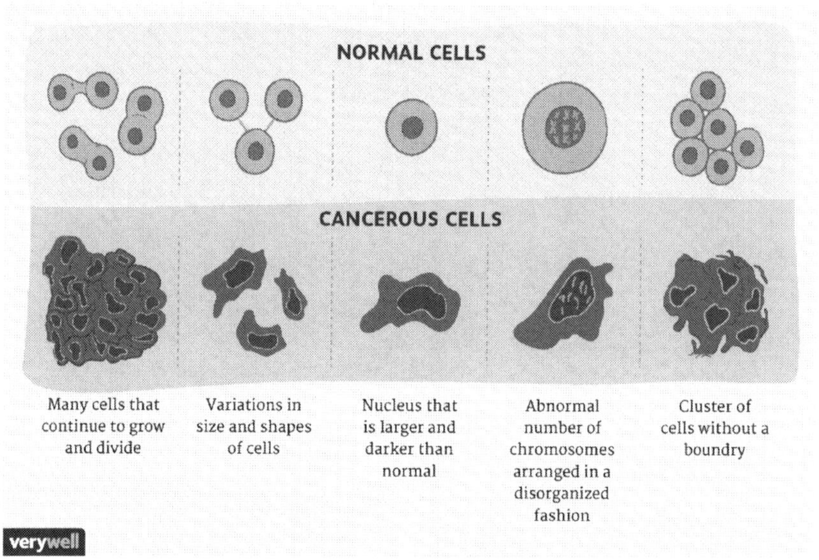

Can we see any correlations between thoughts and cells? Look at the pictures of Dr. Emoto's work. See if you can identify similarities between the "Thank You" and the healthy cell versus "You make me sick, I will kill you." and the cancer cell. I am not trying to make claims of anything health-wise, just pushing the way you think about thoughts and health itself. How is the physical, mental, emotional, and spiritual body all a reflection of each other?

Do you think you can change your molecular structure, energetic frequency, and "vibes" according to thoughts?

Over half of our body is water.

We have between 60,000 and 80,000 thoughts a day.

Masaru Emoto discovered that thoughts have a profound impact on water.

This beginning research on water molecules has extended out to tests on plants, containers of rice, and other fascinating correlations between feelings and their direct effects on the physical world. What does that mean for you and your thoughts? The narcissist can be so frustrating. They know all kinds of little tricks to send you into the land of milk of honey for them - anger, hate, fear, frustration, powerlessness, jealousy, insecurity, self-doubt, and the whole list of negative emotions. You may eventually decide you feel trapped in the relationship and hate them. Ouch! Who's that hurting you or them?

Yet it seems the impossible mission for healers, lovers, and those wired to love bliss, peace, equality, and harmony. Is this possible for us to stay in a state of nirvana or positive emotions while operating here with those wired to survive off feeding the darkness? Seriously how can we take a world run by narcissists and stay in positive emotions?

This would be so much easier if we were all little bliss bubbles running around. On some other higher dimensions, that's what we are doing I'm sure of it. We deeply understand how energy and the spiritual vessel works. We use a complete constant state of LIGHT together with our physical bodies as ways to express LOVE through the arts, music, food, dance, and everything we do. Every present moment becomes an expression of cosmic consciousness separate yet interlaced in beauty with everyone and everything. All that we touch is infused by our universally tapped magic of love and happiness.

We are capable of that here on Earth and will be shifting back into that original vibration as the age of Enlightenment is upon us!

Hold on a minute, though, because we are not there yet. We are on a planet of darkness where none of that sounds easy what-so-ever. Most of it will get much easier, though, as we learn the rules of the game that no one has ever taught us. These so-called "dark forces" need to be here. They show us our weaknesses, imbalances, unhealed wounds, and provide us with the tests of our inner darkness and ego.

When we heal entirely, balance, and jump all the spiritual tests they supply, the tables will completely turn. Not because they have changed but because we have. We have been enlightened and recognize they played a pivotal role in that journey. Every time we drop into lower emotions, narcissistic supply is fed. We can't help but feed the beast when we are unhealed. We must become accountable as the gatekeeper to narcissistic supply.

Toxic people place us in positions of moral dilemmas continually. They make us face aspects of ourselves, our fears, failures, and push us into narcissism ourselves. Our brains are hard-wired to be negative, and dealing with them presents us with choices to follow that wiring or do the rewiring. In breaking through the oppression, healing ourselves, the Earth, and coming together with these opposing forces trying to hold us captive, we will do what we are designed to do. Become stronger emotionally, mentally, physically, and spiritually as we do the soul healing that has been triggered by these games, situations, and different players since the beginning of time!

Just for ease of explanation, pretend the narcissist is your toaster that needs an outlet to work. You have outlets and are an energy center. They need that energy to operate and function. Your outlets are where you have matching inner work or holes in your mental, emotional, or spiritual body that allows them to plug into you. We must do the inner healing to cover the outlets.

This is exactly why going no contact does not work. If you have not learned every valuable piece of vital growth, a new person will come into your life — same issues. Narcissistic supply is negative emotions, feelings, thoughts, and anywhere others have pushed you into the false self or ego. The energetic charges that make up your body are still attracting you back to where you have not yet evolved. Another facet of this is people leave narcissists regularly. They still feed them narcissistic supply even in going "no contact."

I only believe in "no energy" and it doesn't matter if I'm going toe to toe with them voicing my opinion or 100 miles away. To be capable of never feeding the narcissist, you must choose to get involved in your healing. If you're looking for a book to blame, finger point, or put everything on the narcissists, you might as well put this down. If you are looking for the keys to why you keep attracting these situations over and over, continue reading. You have the matching inner wounds and power to stop them dead in their tracks regardless of how you have to interact with them.

This journey keeps evolving deeper and deeper into a sea of soul evolution, where you will begin to see others as merely an extension of yourself. If there is an adverse emotional reaction to anyone in your life, it is seeking to communicate where your healing must be done. Nothing here is about other people. Other people, life situations, and all of these dramas have orchestrated around what is radiating inside you.

What are some techniques that can be accessed to heal?

To unlock these magnetic charges deeply, feel those emotions you've been holding onto for so long. Love and accept yourself with whatever feelings come up. Ask yourself where in my body do I feel this? Decide to let it go from your entire being. You can use visualization to see that happening. Maybe it all drops down into a black hole beneath you. Or you breathe it out and watch it disappear into smoke. This is personally my favorite technique because it's simple and can be done without anyone knowing you're transforming the emotions and energetic charges. Maybe it's in the form of a color with any dark emotions swirling out in black as you breathe out and red being a symbol of love filling you up as you breathe in.

We are all healers internally; it's just awakening what works best for you. EFT (Emotional Freedom Technique) is another tool that provides a solid and easy to use format. This is an energy medicine technique that is very powerful as it works to rewire the body's system on the emotional, physical, energetic, and spiritual levels. If you have access to the internet, you will find a lot of tutorials, information, and step by step directions.

I do like this explanation at https://emofree.com/eft-tutorial/tapping-basics/how-to-do-eft.html, which provides a basic explanation on how to use tapping to deal with negative emotions. If you have internet access you can watch this 8-minute tutorial by clicking this link:

https://www.youtube.com/watch?v=1wG2FA4vfLQ

EFT is a scientifically proven system to help deal with all kinds of traumas in the body. Nick Ortner is another highly recommended author and healer who works with EFT for all sorts of different issues. This is an affiliate link to his website listing all of his books, programs, and resources he has available. When you use these affiliate links, I receive a commission from whatever purchases you may make, which allows us all to help each other! Here is the link:

https://rd117.isrefer.com/go/TTSBookStore/mareckel/

And if you are not in a financial position to purchase anything, these authors and healers have a fantastic amount of free information through blogs, YouTubes, and their webinars.

Whatever method you find resonates with you is not important. What is important is healing places you are divided from yourself and others that are reflecting in the relationship. Ultimately your energetic field will not shift without complete healing. Your thoughts, intentions, and action are the most powerful tool you have, regardless of the method. What could the healed version of you look like?

You love and accept yourself no matter who betrays and abandons you. You will never betray and abandon yourself. (self-partner)

You must love and accept yourself and others unconditionally. (you see others and suffering as messengers)

You must love and accept yourself at this moment where your insecurity is shining. Maybe the narcissist just made you feel stupid. You must love and accept yourself when you're not perfect, make mistakes, or trip in front of the crowd.

Maybe the narcissist doesn't hear your feelings or concerns. Love yourself at that moment. Even when no one else hears me, I listen to myself. My opinions are valid. My feelings are important, and I will voice them.

Maybe they just set you up to feel ashamed of yourself. They are mocking you. Get in your body and feel it. No one can make you feel ashamed unless the comment, scoffs, or attacks hit your internal registers, which means that you feel internally ashamed of yourself. You love yourself based on conditions.

Maybe they just pulled you into their three-ring circus trying to get you to play in their game of anger and finger-pointing. You didn't stand up for yourself, and you feel like a coward. You let them walk all over you, and there you are just left a pile of YUCK-O emotions. You're disappointed in you.

Your boss just mocked you in front of your co-workers. Someone you have worked overtime for unpaid. A person you thought was not only your boss but a friend. The whole office is laughing at you. Are you sensitive about a joke, or did they hit your inner wound? These situations manifest in a thousand ways.

Narcissists are designed on purpose just the way they are to be the messenger of your internal working order that you cannot see. That is precisely why they must be wired to search out and pummel guilt, shame, humiliation, insecurities, weaknesses, and soul wounds. We have to switch our thinking from blaming them to realizing that we are the match. Suffering is by design, so we will be uncomfortable enough to go within and do this deep personal work.

Whatever feelings come up allow them to happen in love and without judgment. Deeply move into them instead of away. Allow yourself to have those feelings and explore what is there like walking straight into a fire. There is a long list of ways that the narcissists are showing you those internal wounds. This is an excellent place of gratitude you can feel for the narcissist as you realize your responsibility in the relationship. They are giving you the road map to your soul wounds.

Think of it like this. We have these cuts on us, but we are blind to them. The narcissist is the personality type that comes up to you and rubs their finger right in it. OUCH! These are exactly how emotional traumas are for all of us. The internal issues are what need to be healed. They make up the cuts and bruises on our hearts, minds, and spirits. Look for how this may go way back into childhood even. If you can start identifying repeat patterns in your life that continue to resurface, you know it's something you have not overstepped, healed, or evolved.

Love yourself no matter who does or doesn't show up for you. I stand up and show up for myself.

Love yourself, regardless of what anyone else does. What other people do or don't do does not make or break me, my self-love, value, and contribution.

Love the imperfect you with flaws and mistakes.

Visualize yourself in some way, and maybe you are a young child feeling abandoned and betrayed. Hug that inner spirit, wounded child, and commit YOURSELF. I will always be here for you. I will always take care of you. I will always love and admire you in your strengths and weaknesses. No one else needs to give you love and approval. You do!

Abandonment and betrayal are an essential part of self-growth. They will be played over and over in our lives until we stand solidly in ourselves. It does not matter what happens; we cannot be shaken. As long as you are up and down, according to someone else, you are their puppet. The narcissist is the expert at pulling your strings. You just haven't figured out yet that the scissors to cut them are right there in your hand.

You are the ONLY one who can do it.

Loving and accepting yourself and others in those messy ways, we are very vulnerably human is essential. When you can acknowledge your inner wounds and own up to yours, you will also accept others when theirs show up. If you cannot realize where these wounds match, you will make judgments and create karma. Karma creates negative emotions and can attract situations back to us. This is also a pivotal cornerstone where we must flip the switch.

Until you reach complete unconditional love, gratitude, forgiveness, and peace with the narcissist, you are not "there" yet. This can only be achieved by recognizing what a beautiful role they have played in your life as the spiritual, mental, and emotional trainer. Think about this in the physical world. You start seeing a personal trainer at the gym. They push you to do ten more push-ups than you think you can do. They add weight to your strength-building sets. During your workouts, you grunt, groan and want to die trying to make it through the sets.

At the end of the six weeks, you check the charts and realize how much stronger they made you. Not because they coddled you at your first sign of weakness. You work harder than if you were alone. That's why we are stronger as a team, but then once everyone gets together, all of these soul triggers start going off. Narcissists are mental, emotional, and spiritual trainers.

Besides, we have this other element where we must see that we are the narcissist. For example, the narcissist zeroes in on someone "love-bombs" and then devalues them. How could we see our guilt in this behavior? Easy. We are people pleasers who will go out of our way to be and do everything for everyone.

At the heart of the narcissist and empath is an insecure wounded child seeking love, approval, validation, and security from other people.

When we have not become the source of love and approval to ourselves, the ego takes over. It is seeking admiration and support, needing to be everything to everyone. Both parties are looking for outside validation and desire so deeply to be everyone's hero. The narcissist may zero in on one particular person to "love bomb" and "idolize," but it's the same issue. Except without the triangles that are created while they elevate someone else, we couldn't see another matching element. Insecurity.

It would not matter if they were married to the God/Goddess themselves; they would not be happy. They appear so confident in many ways, but under the veil is a deeply insecure person. That's precisely why they must magnify their contribution while not acknowledging yours. You have to be able to see where and how you mirror each other to be complete compassion. The new educated version of you goes through all of the phases, tactics, and qualities of the narcissist with new understanding. You identify where you've healed and grown. There is a more profound sense of gratitude, unconditional love, and forgiveness in your heart.

While they are love bombing you, soak it all up. They can be quite funny, endearing, and entertaining. While you are being devalued and discarded, use it as an opportunity to heal and mend. Don't allow anyone's comments, criticisms, anger, or negativity to define or affect you.

Everything that does affect you is a place you still have inner work to do. For them to get any emotional reaction from you, the outside voice has to match the inner voice.

Think of it this way. If you are a millionaire and do not have issues with money, then what happens if a middle-classed citizen calls you "a broke joke." It doesn't affect you one bit. Now let's say it's important to you that everyone knows how much money you have because it's your source of validation, love, security, and approval. This comment has hit your inner wound because you do not want to be seen or thought of like "a broke joke." Once you have healed, the old patterns will resurface, but you will see it as a mirror of your old unhealed self. The situations will allow you to hold them in gratitude and love as they just served their role as your messenger. What is left is no longer your issue together, but the remaining part of what is their problem. There will be no emotional charge or judgments inside of you for them.

During the times when the narcissist discards you, make yourself a priority. They are ignoring you completely and before it bothered you. Now you have lots of interests, friends and are busy with your projects. Maybe they just criticized you all day. They are twisting everything around to try to make you feel ashamed, guilty, insecure, unloved, gaslighted, or a whole list of inner wounds. You never fell into their games.

Powerless becomes powerful.

When you get to this space where these situations no longer bother you, then you realize I have deeply healed! I am no longer a pinball to the narcissist's machine. You can see all of these phases happening and recognize just how much growth they have triggered. You are being gaslighted and decide to stand up for yourself, the truth, and precisely what is going on. They just use triangles of people to create a nicely orchestrated smear campaign. The people-pleaser in you would have been screaming. Now that you are healed and evolved, you do not care what anyone thinks of you. You know who you are and what you stand for regardless of the pack of wolves standing against you.

There is a magnified flow of positive emotions triggered now! It's nothing short of amazing to have turned the tale of the narcissist and the empath. All these invisible bonds that attached us to someone "toxic" were matching where we were "toxic" to ourselves. The new energetic bonds can form with others. I love and support myself can attract people who love and support you. I see not only my weaknesses but my strengths. I can promote myself, and the job comes into play where you get promoted. You see life as a mirror, and you are in charge.

This is an epic space to develop yourself into, and I'm so excited for it to start happening for you!

CHAPTER 7
MONEY MANIPULATIONS

IF YOU HAVE FOUND YOURSELF in a narcissistic relationship, you are positively running dysfunctional programs around money. Narcissists love money. Money is ego validation. Money is control. Money is power. There are a few ways that our personal money traumas can show up in life and these dysfunctional relationships.

For those people who have money, hard work ethic, connections they need, or some valuable possessions, this could manifest in several ways. The fundamental issue may be that you have to be a resource to someone to be loved. Meaning you need to give someone something or provide them with finances, perks, and gifts to feel valuable and deserving of their friendship or relationship. You do not think on your own without giving away "stuff" you deserve love. You are carrying the matching counterpart in this relationship.

Narcissists use people for what they can receive. They saw you and the pencil started to work out exactly how this fits their agenda. Hmmmm financial stability, maybe some property, or an inheritance possibility. You give way more than you take whether it be energy, money, or attention. Narcissist relationships tilt in their favor. Remember who we are talking about here. The snake in the tree of Garden of Eden luring in Adam and Eve.

They are not capable of a real relationship, only in seeing you and your good-hearted nature as a commodity that fits their needs. In fact, they are entirely unrealistic about what is fair in contributing to the relationship. Everything must end up with them having the advantage. They are worth more, deserve the best, and it should all come to them without much effort on their part.

Internally, you must be the opposite match. Everything is a mirror where you carry those inner wounds. You must be a commodity, give treats, ego props, or pay for things to have relationships and friends. With your personality alone, you are not enough. Givers attract takers. Are you tired of one-way street relationships yet?

The perfect person shows up to take, take, and take. And remember, narcissists are wired to make you feel like it's never enough to keep you plugging away, giving more and more. They will shame you for every dollar you spend. You will walk on eggshells about what you do while they feel valid spending money frivolously on their eccentric needs.

Or the opposite situation can occur. The Empath can be the "stay at home" partner who has NO money. Perhaps they are the parent who chooses to be home and raise the kids, or they get an illness that forces them out of being able to work. Maybe they have a family business together, and the narcissist has all the control. There are many ways a narcissist can weed into our lives and take over the finances. Lots of different games and power plays happen.

They will play games, manipulate, and twist all situations around money. You may think they are a fantastic provider. Yet, some things don't match up — one moment they are giving. Perhaps you worked a lot of overtime unpaid. You have a big project due. They show up when you are at your wits end with a "bonus." Mind you, it's not what you deserve, but it's enough to keep you going.

Covert narcissists can be a bit confusing to figure out. Sometimes the masks and illusions can be tricky, but we know something is wrong at our core. During the love bombing the gifts maybe over the top or they will take you out to fancy dinners. Once you commit to them, they start to shame you for every dollar you spend.

In romantic partners where each person holds a job and contributes to the family bills, the narcissist will always try to get an angle on more of the money. They will twist things to manipulate you to pay more than your fair share. At one moment, they could be "love bombing" you with appearing generous. The next minute they are twisting things to make you feel guilty. Or they will consistently throw in comments about what you should pay, get them, or turn situations to keep you giving to their advantage.

Internally at a soul level, you have attracted this counterpart. When we look at everything backward, we can see what is inside of us. This is the key to the next level of consciousness. New kinds of thinking and questioning into our relationships show us a new set of questions. How is this about me? How is this trying to show me my qualities? We put ourselves back into power by discontinuing blaming and finger pointing them.

Think about your job, relationship partner, or perhaps it's a family member or some other triangle that locks you into a money pattern that creates suffering. I will throw a lot of things out there. You will need to do some self-assessing here.

Ask yourself a lot of questions.

How do I view money, and what belief systems do I have about it?

Were there any issues in my family while I was growing up that centered on money?

Do I get anxiety about confrontations around money? (perhaps instead of standing up for what is right, I pay the extra or give in to the narcissist to avoid "fighting")

Can I receive without feeling I have to give back?

Do I feel guilty when others spend money on me?

Do I feel like I have to spend money on others to be liked?

Do I feel guilty when I spend money on myself?

Do I feel like I truly deserve to be spoiled?

Do I feel like I'm not good enough or worth it?

Do I believe the universe has enough for everyone, or do I live in scarcity (there is never enough)?

Do I link spending money with stress or happiness?

How do I feel if I have to ask someone else for help?

We have internal issues that match up and reflect the opposite side of the narcissist coin. They, on the other hand, have the opposing viewpoints on money. Here's how a narcissist thinks about money, gifts, and resources that come to them.

I can receive feeling no type of need to give back.

People in my life are only beneficial if they are a commodity or resource to me. There must be some financial gain, ego props, or energetic feedback they will supply for my inflated ideals of myself.

I have no guilt about others spending money on me.

I deserve everything.

I am worth all the treasures in the universe.

I believe life will bring me everything I dream of and more.

I am not capable of having empathy for people, so I do not get emotionally involved by feeling guilty when they spend money. Money is a source of happiness for me, not guilt and stress.

All situations should be assessed, manipulated, and twisted for my needs.

The laws of attraction have proven that what we believe and think manifests in reality. The narcissist is a great teacher for us to realize exactly how these rules work. Energetically what is inside of us physically appears in the world. By energetically, I mean what we believe, think, and internally feel at the core of our soul shows up. Have you ever watched a narcissist achieve things that defy your mind? They are entirely unrealistic about life. They have dreams and visions that we are mystified by, yet what happens? These outlandish goals show up for them.

We are so grounded in the here and now. We doubt what can happen and what's possible. Ideas get created from these dysfunctional internal patterns. I'm not good enough. I'll never get anywhere. I couldn't ever have that. We unknowingly block our goals and dreams. Narcissists fulfill their goals and dreams by trusting themselves and the universe. Even if they are egomaniacs, they wholeheartedly believe in themselves. They trust in their abilities, talents, and gifts. This shows us an important lesson. Our thought patterns can either support or destroy us. These are qualities that are keys to us reaching the sky, and we can use some lessons from narcissists. Ha!

I am trying to pack a lot of concepts into this book, so I want to give you some additional resources to expand your knowledge. Christie Marie Sheldon has a beautiful YouTube video that perhaps is the best representation I have ever seen to explain belief systems clearly. In 30 minutes, she beautifully outlays the key concepts in an easy-to-understand format. If you have internet access, I highly recommend watching the presentation. It is titled, "Change Your Energetic Frequency To Change Your Reality – Christie Marie Sheldon Free Training."

Here is the link: https://www.youtube.com/watch?v=zn7ZxZjNLro

The universe wants us all to live abundantly. All the resources are here for us. We must work through these crucial parts of ourselves that we haven't yet healed. Do you believe you are going to work forever for peanuts? Well, it looks like you need a narcissist to live out that belief system so you can work away for very little your whole life. Listen to your thoughts and what you continually say about money. We are born with all the necessary skills to heal into abundance in all ways, once we understand the concepts.

What most people do is get a full load of resentment, bitterness, envy, and hate. The wrong people keep getting all the money, material stuff, and power. Why is the narcissist getting everything they want while the empath is slaving away for crumbs? Now you know why. You have all of these imbalances, dysfunctional belief systems, wounded parts, and failed spiritual tests running the TV show called "your life". You can solve these inner issues though.

There are several different elements at play that need to be addressed.

What beliefs do we have about money?

What emotions come up around your finances?

How secure, confident, and deserving of financial abundance do you feel?

Are you jealous and envious of people who have money?

Perhaps you have lots of money, but feel you need to buy things for others to be liked?

One we haven't fully covered is the spiritual tests. Will we make a stand for ourselves? This can show up in so many ways as they seem to have control of your survival. Will that trigger fear and insecurity within you? You may love your job and the people but hate the way your boss treats you. Are you feeling cornered into staying in the slave/slave master situation? You don't believe in yourself, place value on what you do, and fear how you will survive. The universe must have consequences for these inner weaknesses.

In your mind, the narcissist is putting a roof over your head and paying the bills. You may have a business relationship that requires you to keep being their puppet because financially, you need them as clients. If we don't start understanding these concepts, we will blame them or life or whatever. Money is simply the tool necessary to corner you into suffering, so you will finally work on YOU.

Self-anger, frustration, powerlessness, and so many negative emotions can show up as internally we know we are "selling" our soul. We are right. We are all whores to our fears, insecurities, weaknesses, and ego. Money becomes a factor of control and hate in our lives. Is it about the money or the fact we hate the part of us that doesn't make a stand for ourselves? Is fear-based thinking standing in our way? We believe we need to play their game to survive financially. Setting boundaries, honoring ourselves, and following our personal truths isn't comfortable when there's some way our security is locked into and controlled by them.

Narcissists also create illusions around money. They gaslight us. We are naïve and gullible, so we don't see how this is happening. We don't investigate if their words line up with their actions. Narcissists will brainwash you into lots of little games to keep you spending as little money as possible on yourself while spending more money on themselves. Even tilting the past and making up stories. We need to start paying attention.

For example, this could be a talk about tightening up the budget? They focus all the energy on what you are doing and blow it out of proportion but minimize the money they spend. If your boss is a narcissist, they will appear to be making it, but just barely. As much as they would love to give you a raise, they can't "afford" to right now. In a business relationship, they will keep raising fees in little places. Like taxes, small tiny increments that wouldn't cause a huge uproar but are significantly chipping away at how much money you get. With a spouse, it's the same game of working you over for financial gain, just a little different delivery.

They are always working the little guy over to take more and more for themselves. We are a total match because we don't step up to the plate, put our foot down, and make them accountable. Somehow, your scenario with the narcissist fits into this grand game, whether you have money, have no money, or share expenses with them. The same tactics, manipulations, lies, and twisted perspective are just part of the plan to create that suffering we need.

Narcissists are geared to make poor decisions with money so it will get under your skin. Maybe you have watched them spend money on things they qualify as necessary even though it's irrational, self-centered, and eccentric. They will buy top of the line expensive items but can't afford a raise or something for you. You will try to scrimp and save to be flabbergasted when they buy some frivolous things.

Take your power and control back.

Set boundaries.

Face your insecurities and weaknesses.

Find out who you are and the authentic gifts you want to pursue.

Pass the spiritual tests.

Let's talk about the spiritual tests and our own inner narcissist. Your whole life is a set-up, orchestrated by all of these invisible inner workings. We just need to open our eyes to all of these elements that keep us trapped into repeat patterns of suffering. When you truly connect to yourself, you will see your own inner narcissist. Of course, it may need a little push from the true narcissist but it's so important to see. For example, the office jerk just got the job promotion you wanted. Do you become bitter, resentful, jealous, or envious as they roll in the material world items? Doesn't it make it so challenging to genuinely be happy for them and admire all the "goodies" that come into their life? The narcissist in them is pushing the narcissist in you.

You have to see your own guilt in operating just like they do. If you cannot see your own narcissistic qualities you make judgments of them rather than forgive and unconditionally love others who are bitter, hateful, or jealous of you. See your inner beast. Acknowledge and accept that dark side of you. Then you can easily turn all of these situations around.

I know we often think we are irritated with others but really, we are just aggravated with ourselves. Next time something that deals with money, promotions, gifts, or financial perks along with a narcissist look inside of you. Think of all the emotions you feel? If you are still locked into them, see, accept, and acknowledge the negative reactions. Unconditionally love yourself with your hate, bitterness, anger, jealousy, etc. How can you see others trapped in the dynamics and unconditionally love them without seeing your own guilt? Think of the concepts we have talked about and how the office narcissist got the promotion.

They believe in themselves, do you?

They know that all of the gifts of the universe should show up at their door, do you?

They are very capable of acknowledging their contributions to the company, can you?

Are you able to make decisions, or indecisive?

Did you even put in for the promotion or are you expecting them to notice you?

Do you really want power and control or do you like being invisible and having smaller responsibilities?

At some point, if you do self-work, you will be the one with the promotion, living in abundance, and following your dreams. Someone may be jealous, bitter, envious, and hate you. Most likely, it will be a narcissist. They really can't be happy for other people. Instead of making judgments about them, you see them with complete compassion, unconditional love, and forgiveness. You have been in their shoes.

It's really fascinating being awake and watching the reality show go down. You get to the point of being complete compassion at all times. No one is at fault here. Everyone is just being the messenger to each other of all of these elements. In its dysfunction is a specific divine function.

There are so many ways for this game to play out. They could be the opposite, a complete tightwad watching every nickel and dime. You can't afford to do fun stuff. Everything is a full breakdown to the penny until any entertainment gets ruined. Fun costs money. Entertainment often includes other people, and they are not the complete focus. That's challenging for a narcissist.

Or they won't spend their own money but use you for your generosity while they watch their savings account go up, up, and up. You probably have no clue about how much money they have. All the ways they contribute are inflated. They exaggerate dollars and cents. If it was $100 spent towards something, they say it was $200.

Maybe you have the child-like narcissist, which in some aspects this is what we adore about them. Yet, when it comes to money, they will buy the big, shiny ego validating objects when your kids need shoes. They love the show and are completely engrossed in appearances and material world items for themselves. There is no practicality here. As logical people who live in reality, we are that opposite mirror.

Until you work out all of your issues around money, you are the match! Empaths and narcissists are opposite ends of the tipping scales.

When we learn how to balance our internal dysfunctional working order, we will manifest our desires plus create value and supporting relationships with the people around us. We aren't looking to be narcissists but just balance ourselves. They could use some of our qualities and we could use some of theirs.

Let's do a little breakdown here of how we can use this relationship to do self-work and balance our internal running programs to finally self-heal. Here's what narcissists can teach us by showing us the world is a mirror. Their internal working order is...

- Open to receiving all the universe has to offer. Their internal belief systems say I am more than good enough. I have a higher value than other people. I blow up and inflate my strengths and cannot see, accept, or acknowledge my weaknesses. The people they attract do exactly that, propping them up on the pedestal. They at a soul level fully know people, money, and situations will show up for their greatness. The world should come delivered on a silver platter. We watch it happen.
- They are unrealistic and have grandiose ideas they ultimately believe in fully. The universe delivers. You do not see them laying in self-doubts, worry, anxiety, or stress about the details or need to figure out exactly how it will happen.

The unhealed Empath most likely has internal wiring that is something like this...

Have difficulty receiving, guilt, shame, or stress all connected to money in some way. Self-doubts, insecurities, and weaknesses we blow up in our mind while never giving ourselves credit, seeing, or acknowledging our strengths. We place a higher value and trust in other people rather than ourselves.

We do not believe the world should show up for us on a platter. Our realistic minds must pencil out grandiose ideas, so we do not believe in them. The how's, why's, and what's need an explanation. We rationalize rather than trust in the universe, and it's magic.

We have a servant's mindset. The worker bee's that don't want the power and control. We would rather show up and sweep the floor. The pressure of the CEO chair doesn't fit us. There is so much manipulation by the narcissist's' demands and how they twist things. We fall right into their hands by having this imbalance ready to serve, self-sacrifice, and "save." Let me do this for you.

The opposites reflect the keys to each other in the relationship. Narcissists do not link money to stress unless they are trying to twist it to make you feel guilty. Which they love to do, but it's on purpose to show you where you have dysfunctional programs running about money. No one can put guilt or shame on us unless it's already inside of us. Without them being wired that way, they cannot show you the crossed wire you have they are reflecting. You feel guilty or ashamed of spending money on yourself, or however, this shows up.

These are all ideas meant to make you think. What are my fundamental issues about money that are triggered? Yours may have manifested differently, but we can easily find the messages. The narcissist has good and bad qualities, just like we do. I want to take some lessons here from them on the good. Note that does not mean twisting reality, using people as commodities, or creating illusions to corner more money, resources, and energy for yourself. That means something more along the line of balancing the scales…

NARCISSIST: I see money as a tool to buy resources for myself and create happiness.

EMPATH: I see money as evil, creating suffering for people and myself.

NARCISSIST: I deserve everything and more.

EMPATH: I don't deserve anything.

NARCISSIST: I make great decisions, love power, control, and do not see errors in myself.

EMPATH: I question my decisions, have a hard time making them, would rather not be in power or control of others, and all I see are errors in myself.

NARCISSIST: Great at manifesting because they are unrealistic.

EMPATH: Hold themselves back from goals and dreams by being overly realistic, blocking the magic of the universe.

NARCISSIST: Completely unaccountable.

EMPATH: Overly accountable.

NARCISSIST: People are simply a tool for me to extract money, resources, and energy.

EMPATH: I must be a tool supplying money, resources, or energy to others to be loved.

We need to find the middle line between the narcissist and us. We are here in a physical body to use our relationships with life, people, money, and all situations so we can work on ourselves. The reality is all of our energies are connected and work together to show each other our internal trauma. Nothing here is about other people.

Where are narcissists showing you what needs to be healed, addressed, and balanced?

Are they tilting your perspective about money? Or is the tilted perspective, unhealed wounds and trauma's inside of you just being played out in your reality? They are the messenger. What would happen if you pulled the plug on the part of you that is working overtime to make other people happy, or healed the part of you that has a difficult time receiving? Do you get anxiety when you have to stand up for yourself, and what is fair around money? Could you identify in your soul where you fit into these categories and start doing the inner work to balance the scales?

Absolutely!

The narcissist will do their job by making this challenging. You are going to have to stand up for yourself in their game of charades. They will not like this new you who has resolved your inner imbalances. The intimidation, gaslighting, and manipulation tools will get bumped up. Being solid in yourself despite all of their techniques and head games requires inner work. Trusting, having faith, and honoring yourself may trigger fear. If it's your boss, what if they fire this new you? Or how will your partner react?

If you're married to a narcissist know their go-to move is your fear. For example, the first thing a narcissist may love to do is pull the abandonment and betrayal game. They love to either threaten to leave or kick you out. You have just stood your ground, voiced your opinion, or made a stand that doesn't fit into their reality. This aspect of their personality tests us. Do you have any fear within you? Can you make it on your own? Are you a solid sense of support to yourself or squirming with anxiety and feeling co-dependent?

Take a few moments right now to look at your situations with money. Be honest with yourself. Find out exactly where you're holding the key to being the imbalanced partner in this relationship. Are you angry, bitter, or resentful? Is it because of them, or your scales are tipped? On the outside, you will think it is the money, boss, spouse, or whoever you feel has control over the financial aspect of your life. On the inside, it's been about you all along.

Balancing the internal scales is a massive awakening, and that requires unraveling ourselves.

Finding these mirrors and imbalances is an essential first step, but we need to complete the list to see all the elements at play. Use this list to help you break down all issues into parts, like a checklist.

1. Is this an out of balance element of myself?
2. Is the narcissist mirroring me?
3. Do I have belief systems that are making this come true?
4. What kinds of judgments have I made to create this?
5. Is this something I reject or hate about myself?
6. Is this a failed spiritual test?

We have looked at several of these items. Let's discuss judgments, self-rejection, and failed spiritual tests intensely. Beyond these little out-of-balance registers, something else happens. We find a lot of hate. Let's see I need my narcissistic boss and this crappy job to pay my bills. Or I need my marriage because they are putting a roof over my head and my children's. What will happen if I leave emotionally with the children? How will I support myself? Maybe it's a family relationship that you are cornered into staying or living with a relative.

Judgments of them, judgements of us, judgments of everything in between. We are the judge, jury, and executioner.

What happens when we stay in a job we don't like because it's a paycheck we need? What happens when we stay in a relationship we don't like for financial stability? What happens when we cower to our internal fears of stepping out on our own? What happens as we continually rate ourselves in this material world? A lot of negative emotions start rolling. The subconscious is creating the suffering we need to check out of the internal dysfunctions.

Are we living in a miserable "comfort zone"? Do we know deep in our core what is happening and hate ourselves for staying? Not only do we reject ourselves, but we are afraid of stepping out onto our own. Fear! Powerlessness! Self-Doubt! The universe has lined up the perfect spiritual test by this personality type having control. Still, we have no faith in ourselves or whoever you call the creator to take care of us.

Even if you decide to leave the narcissist if you are aware of their personality you cannot simply tell them. You need to put things in order and change directions quietly, and it maybe while you are living with them or working for them. Now you are the liar and manipulator. Their qualities have cornered you into being "them".

Do you see why negative emotions are essential and that we can end our love affair with them by self-healing?

We need those negative emotions. We need suffering. Our natural instinct is to make excuses for our faults and twist things to make others accountable. HMMMMM, who does that sound like? The narcissist. Yes.

We have to recognize our inner narcissist now. We have been guilty of the same things they do. Hahaha! The higher self, subconscious, or inner voice is honest with us, knows all we can be, and controls our whole show. Yet, it's the hardest voice to hear because the ego likes to shout so loud, blaming all of our "stuff" on other people. The ego feeds us with lies and makes excuses to stay in the comfort zone.

That's what's soooo AMAZING about the creator's design program!

The narcissist is the catalyst for so much personal growth. People stay in jobs with bosses they hate, marriages, living arrangements, and business relationships all because they are afraid. They won't be able to survive without the narcissist. FEAR! And narcissists love us living in fear, powerlessness, self-doubt, and feeling out of control.

It's our choice to stand in our way or powerfully create. Until then, the wrong people have the power, money, and are the decision makers because the right people are busy living in their fears, self-doubts, insecurities, and comfort zones. We need narcissists to create the suffering necessary for us to address and heal these issues. For this to happen, there needs to be a complete rewiring of our internal matching dysfunctional systems.

We must face the fears that get triggered by stepping away from the narcissists instead of staying in the comfort zone. This includes those imbalances and weaknesses, plus we have to jump the spiritual tests. When the narcissist gets the job promotion, a fancy car, money, or control of the resources, go ahead and admire them. There is more than enough in the universe for all of us to live abundantly.

Besides you wouldn't get triggered into jealousy and envy by a nice, good hearted, hard-working person getting all the resources, money, and ego validation. All of us who want to see things be fair, according to moral values, skills, and hard work ethics want to scream. Why is that self-centered egomaniac just stepping into great deals while I'm slaving away barely making it? But that's another necessary test they supply. Will we get bitter, hard-hearted, jealous, and angry or stay in high vibes like admiration even if the "asshole" gets the dream job we always wanted?

If we fall into the traps of the ego, we become the narcissist. Yet, we have to see our guilt in being the narcissist to love others unconditionally. That way, we don't make judgments and create karma. I know I'm making the same point several times but I want you to understand all of the elements fully.

Let's look at a case study to identify precisely how this can be accomplished.

CASE STUDY #864: ANNE CATALIN

I think it's easy to shuffle ourselves, our goals, dreams, and visions. When it comes to a mother and her children a whole new person shows up. Love is a powerful mover and shaker in our lives. My son showed a lot of natural ability as a baseball player. He wanted to get on a competition team. The money involved in traveling, training, and competing before would have seemed way out of my league. I most likely would have just jumped in the "we can't" wagon if my love for him hadn't pushed me to find a place of...

"We can! I just need to find the way."

I have no problem denying myself anything. I started to understand in my soul work that I can give but have a difficult time receiving. I will stand up for and easily spend money on my kids. That was the fighting element.

Funny too, I used this experience to heal my subconscious, limiting belief systems. My mind would want to wander off stressing about this new financial burden that hadn't even come up yet. I was subconsciously creating stories or excuses for why we couldn't take on this endeavor. Honestly, the big financial part of traveling hadn't hit the checking account. I was just PRE-STRESSING.

Why? Every time that negative self-talk showed up, I made sure to breathe her out, watch that part of me disappear like smoke, and breathe in the positive self-talk. I never realized how many comments and negative dramas I was subconsciously rolling around about money. Do you know what I figured out too? My life had arranged itself in such a way that I was still that little girl who had no control over money. Only guess what my husband was the new controller. And guess who was the controller before that… my ex-husband… before that, my parents!

How many times am I going to hate myself, feel frustrated, and powerless for not having control over money? *(These are repeat patterns around money that you should look for in your life. The people and life situations may change, but the underlying feelings and emotions are the same.)*

I've been doing a lot of self-healing now, and I took a new route. This particular day we went for a walk. I felt this was an excellent time to bring up the competition team while we were walking, holding hands, and discussing life. I started listening intently to his drawn-out explanation of why we shouldn't put our son on the competition team.

We have the money for all the things he needs. Yet when it comes to everyone else, he makes excuses and limits. All the time, he talks about paying off things and tightening up the budget while he spends tons of money on himself. We run our family business around his passion, so all the things he wants to buy are qualified as "for the business". We scrimp and save while he buys what he qualifies as needs. It's so frustrating worrying about how much you spend on groceries while he goes out and buys some new top of the line equipment. When something new shows up that anger, jealousy, and resentment start swirling around and calling me! *(This is a failed spiritual test, and will hold you in its pattern until you can switch the emotions out of ego.)*

Before, I had always allowed him to make me so frustrated. I felt so powerless, having so little control. I didn't want to be this girl. I wanted to be the girl with all the money so I could make my own choices. I wanted to give my son everything, but I wanted to pay for it myself. I hated my life had evolved to this place where I had to ask him for the money. Having children and deciding to stay home with them had been the ruler in my heart that over-weighed the financial perks of a career, but it also led me to have "issues." *(We are always attracting back to us what we "hate" through the laws of attraction.)*

I had done self-work and became very conscious of every situation where my emotions dropped. I used breathing techniques to switch the energy. Every breath out, I would watch those fears, frustrations, and illusions get pulled from every part of my body. Each inhale, I would breathe in unconditional love for myself exactly as I was feeling in that moment. Not the empowered me but the "little me" just wishing I had my own damm money and lots of it!

The real me that's who this is about and reflecting. I'm rejecting this powerless girl every time something comes up that involves money. Since I have divided myself from love, guess what I keep creating or blocking? I block myself from having my own money. I keep creating new situations of the same problem. Over and over and over. Besides that, I was utterly failing the spiritual test that these personalities provide. I was falling into anger, jealousy, and resentment. I did not understand these inner dysfunctional patterns had been creating money and success blocks.

You know what else I had to get accountable. These people in my life were just my messengers for where I was angry at myself. Would it have been easy to love me if I was swimming in my power to make all the money I needed? Yes, but here I was using situation after situation to wake myself up to where I'm divided from my self-love.

This issue didn't start with my husband; it started way back when I was growing up. Honestly, my biggest goal in life was to make enough money that my parents would no longer have to stress about how to pay bills or afford this game called life. I watched my dad STRESS non-stop as a business owner about how everything would get paid. We are business owners, now we stress about how things get paid. Repeat pattern.

I had a great family. No one ever made me feel guilty for the costs of things. I was involved in a LOT of clubs and adventures that all cost money. Internally, I knew money created stress. I guilted myself. Other than money being the source of unhappiness in my mind, my family was perfect.

I had created connections spending money equals STRESS, so try not to spend money. Spending money on me made me feel GUILT, so I pushed money, resources, and gifts away. I assumed because that my relationship with money was other peoples and completely stripped the joy out of receiving. Being a business owner and entrepreneur creates STRESS, ANXIETY, and WORRY. Don't be a business owner or pursue your dreams. Take the "safe" path.

Totally a backward program! Most rich people view money as guess what?!?

HAPPINESS

They don't have an emotional connection to money besides using it as a tool. My emotions about money were ALL negative. The controlling factor of people I loved. The root of all evil and creator of suffering between the have and have nots. My situations in my life just continued to mirror those internal feelings. Everything in my reality just continued to have money operating in my life at this emotional level of "hate, powerlessness, frustration"! Think about this for yourself for a minute... How do you feel about money? What repeat situations can you see that keep popping up, creating triangles in all your relationships with people and money?

Healing involves assessing where your feelings get triggered into negativity. Are there repeating patterns you can identify that have carried from your childhood into adulthood? With Anne, her dad was a business owner and stressed about money. Now her husband was a business owner and stressed about money. Anne rejected herself at a base level, knowing she had given her power away by the narcissist being in complete control of the finances. Love for herself based on conditions versus unconditional love.

A shift in energy around herself and money have to happen before any financial success came into her life. She started to focus on loving herself in those moments where the self-hatred would show up. Not the person she wants to be. The person she wants to be is powerful and has control of the money! She is a rock star who can make her own choices. The broken little girl inside of her still having to "ask" can I do this? The part of herself that feels powerless and entirely out of control is screaming. Her soul mate partner is just creating the right dynamics to show her this space.

We orchestrate everyone and everything in our universe around us.

Let's continue with Anne's story and see how her newly awakened self-healing personality handled the situation differently:

Before this awakening, I would have gotten depressed after this walk. Life would have confined me to thinking I hated him or the money itself. That 10-minute conversation would have rolled around and around repeatedly. I would have listened, followed, and been defined by his decision. My son wouldn't have gotten on the competition team, just creating more anger inside me. Especially when I watched him buy some frivolous item.

However, he's not the issue… if I left him today and I don't heal this space inside myself, I will re-create it with someone else or some other way in my life. This is my inner trauma and my life, my world, and my reality is molding around these wounds so I can finally heal. Who knows how many lifetimes I've been in this repeat situation with different soul mates?

I realized something powerful about narcissists too. There is always enough money for the stuff they want. They have some knowledge to share. They believe they deserve everything. The world should show up for them, and so it does. My natural order was to live in a reality where money is a struggle, stressful, and I doubt the power of the magical place we live in to bring everything to us.

What I am saying here is his thoughts to me about the "we can't" wagon are precisely what fits into my belief systems. My inner voice was being echoed back to me. The emotions he triggered inside me were replays over and over and over to my inner workings. Now is the time to switch the programming. I am more conscious and aware of exactly how I and the universe work.

I got our son enrolled on the competition team, trusting the universe will open up the way. Everything will fall in place for all the money we need and even more. I did healing work right there at the moment and unconditionally loved myself as I am feeling "powerless, frustrated, and angry." This is the most important step, loving ourselves as we are in those messy ways, we reject ourselves.

Then I pulled these negative feelings out of my body in every situation where it showed up. My favorite way to transform emotions is to watch all the negative thought patterns, and limiting belief systems be pulled out of every part of my body and then watch them disappear into smoke.

When I breathe in the incoming oxygen is unconditional love, forgiveness, bliss, and faith. All the unlimited belief systems replace whatever I found to be negative. "I can't. There is not enough." becomes "I can. The universe is abundant."

My mind naturally wants to run negative patterns, blame others, and create stories to validate my powerlessness. It's a conscious effort to keep it on task. Before this whole talk would have turned my mood! But for the first time, I loved myself and the situation exactly as it was rather than rejecting and hating myself. Why don't I have my own money, so I don't have to ask him? I let all the emotions come up, but I kept the loving vibes going through the storm rather than negative vibes for myself, him, and money.

I noticed my narcissist husband setting me up too. He has a drone he wants to buy that cost $10,000, which is not something we need. I mean, really if we can't afford the competition team is a big, fancy drone on the list?!? But when it's something he wants; we have the money. When it's something for someone else, we don't have the money. It's a big game of lies, manipulations, and gaslighting to keep me from spending any money. This was an inner match for me before because I lived in this scarcity mindset.

There is not enough.

The narcissist creates the illusion there is not enough so he can secure more for himself. I would fall for it, believe him, and did not want to fight or create waves for what I felt was fair. *(Can't set boundaries, avoid confrontation, not good enough, don't deserve)* Besides, I'm the "stay at home" parent here. I should sacrifice, right?!? *(Anne disqualified her contribution, and so did the narcissist. Mirrors.)* Shuffling myself was easier than facing any confrontation. I hate arguments and people upset with one another.

If I were reeling in my money, success, and powerfulness, I would not care one bit if he got something new and eccentric. However, being in this position has taught me of my envy, jealousy, bitterness, and resentment. There would be no way for me to see the narcissist within myself. Until I can jump this spiritual hurdle, I need this powerless position to show me how my ego is running my show.

I am a commodity for him because I'm moldable and shapeable. All the head trips, games, and manipulations that were going on never even occurred to me. I never thought that I had guilt and shame about money. It was a brand-new concept. All of this was beautifully and profoundly eye-opening. A new sense of power rushed over me. By changing my inner world that had gone unseen, the outer world would reflect the evolved, healed state of being.

My wheels had fit the narcissists and attracted the relationship. I was the one who was shapeable, walked on eggshells for the Nazi leaders, and spent very little money because of a lack mindset. The narcissist was the match to what internally was going on inside of me. Moving out of this program means clearing out all the negative running programs, emotions, and dysfunctional emotional triggers. Also, there's that fear that I must work through in standing for myself, making me a priority, and deciding to invest in myself. They will not make it easy for us to test our strength and conviction in ourselves.

That's precisely how narcissists are designed perfectly. We have hit so many concepts all in one situation belief systems, imbalances, mirrors, judgments, and spiritual tests. Let's move away from Anne and talk about one more concept. The spiritual test of FAITH or FEAR.

Money is a resource for food, housing, and necessary for survival. Standing for ourselves and setting boundaries when they have the dangling treasured item connected to our livelihood or our hearts may create FEAR. If your financial security or heart (kids, hobbies, etc.) has ties to a narcissistic boss, spouse, or relationship, you will face possibly losing everything. What if you stand up for yourself, your beliefs, and what is right?

Trust and have faith that being true to yourself, healing, and making healthy decisions will allow your destiny to unfold for the highest good. If your mind wants to wander, creating a negative thought pattern. See the thoughts, let them go, and replace them with the positive rewiring.

The biggest monster is the one in our minds. The universe is abundant, and there are no limits.

In a relationship with a narcissist who wants to control everything, money is just a tool. Allow yourself to shift your thinking from them being at fault to "what is my internal cracks?" reflecting in this relationship. From Anne's story, you can see how her internal barometer was swinging along with the narcissist. See where you need to heal and what games or manipulations you need to see through.

The narcissist will make you feel guilty for spending money. Guess what? They match that internal barometer. "I feel guilty about spending money on myself. I deserve nothing. I can't accept or receive." All those running programs you have control over. When you heal through this experience, those comments won't affect you anymore. The narcissist will try to throw their tactics at you, but you won't emotionally react. That's a golden moment!

They will create a false sense of lack to secure more money for themselves. The government and narcissist's favorite game is manipulating things so they can trigger us. You can get smart about the tools they use. You've always fallen in their traps unknowingly, but guess what you know the tactics now. They are laying out the mental land mines, feeding the scarcity mindset. There is not enough. Will you keep stepping into it?

"Most people are deeply scripted in what I call Scarcity Mentality. They see life as having only so much, as though there were only one pie out there. And if someone were to get a big piece of the pie, it would mean less for everyone else." – Stephen Covey

Switching ourselves from a scarcity or lack mindset to an abundance mindset takes self-work. You will need to see through those comments, criticisms, and fit throwing that will come after you. Then stand your ground. They want to make you feel uncomfortable to go against the grain. You are the only one who can decide not to take those emotions on for yourself. For example, after Anne got her son enrolled on the baseball team, the narcissist bumped up his game. She noticed a hurling of NEGATIVE comments meant to shape her against her decision.

This is precisely how the narcissist provides us with the ultimate test. They don't make it easy on purpose. Otherwise, you would never have to get completely solid in yourself. If there's any trickle of unhealed wounds, self-doubt, guilt, or insecurity in you, they will trigger it, and then you can continue to do the work you need to do. You will stand firmly in yourself without dropping into negative emotions regardless of what they do when you achieve the soul healing they are triggering.

No one can make you do anything in terms of emotional abusers and manipulators. You are in charge of exactly what you take on for yourself. Do narcissists feel guilty about spending all the money on themselves? No, they have entirely validated why and how it fits their needs. Besides, they deserve everything to show up without having to put in their fair share. Ask yourself the next time resources, money, or something is twisted by the narcissist to guilt or shame you. What is your issue they are trying to highlight?

Truly making a stand for yourself doesn't always involve walking away but being right there under the firing gun. The narcissist is the exact trainer you need to point out your issues painfully. Learning to know the difference is crucial in reaching that state of nirvana. Every time the narcissist rattles your cage, be grateful, they are your messenger.

When we know how to seal off transferring any energy to the narcissists, there will be no choice for them but to disengage from relationships with us. There is no energy, resources, or commodities there, and you've become a robust force to make sure they are contributing what is fair. We also will have passed all the spiritual tests that are created by these triangles. Plus, you will know all the dynamics to be in relationships with them without losing your energy or letting them drain you physically, mentally, emotionally, or spiritually.

They are specially programmed to provide us with so many tests. They are master manipulators in the game of money, but we are the perfect pawns. We feel guilty about receiving money. We don't stand up for our boundaries. We don't make choices to fight for ourselves and what is right, so we hand them the keys to owning us. Being enslaved to their systems creates a lot of self-anger, frustration, powerlessness, and hatred. Stepping outside of their systems takes faith and self-work.

We have to use this outside world to take personal notes and follow through… Put the time, energy, and soul revelations into motion. There are lessons to be learned from the narcissist on money and reality. Use them as an invaluable tool and insight into yourself.

Becoming perfectly balanced might look something like this…

Money is a tool to create happiness and spread abundance. The more I have, the more I can share with myself and others.

I can give and receive in harmony.

I can take an objective view of life and make decisions that promote the greater good for all.

I can see my strengths and weaknesses. They will voice any places you have self-doubt or insecurities. Once you have over-stepped them, you won't emotionally react only see the inner progress you have made by using the relationship as the key. This increases your love and gratitude for them, rather than expanding into hatred, anger, or bitterness.

I am realistic but also open to the magic of the universe.

I know when to accept responsibility and when to let go because others are trying to make me accountable for their faults.

I have over-stepped all fear, envy, jealousy, and the lack mindset within myself. There is more than enough for everyone. If the narcissist gets the promotion, fancy material items, or steps into a great deal, I will admire and be happy for them. I have jumped all the spiritual tests that narcissistic relationships create by no longer falling into ego — fear, anger, jealousy, envy, powerlessness, resentment, etc.

The power has been in your hands all along. You need to access the knowledge and utilize the tools to create your heaven on earth. The universe will place you in these situations. The choice is always yours.

Repeat or Evolve.

CHAPTER 8
SHOCK AND INTIMIDATION

NARCISSISTS USE SHOCK and intimidation as a tactic to control us. While we are taken off guard and completely distracted by their nonsensible behaviors, they can shape and mold us. It is a fear-based system that works very well for them. Hitler and ISIS are prime examples of a toxic regime utilizing this concept to control.

People do not have a choice on what they think or believe. If they have their own thoughts, ideas, or seek freedom, they face extreme consequences. Cruel and inhumane acts of terrorization punish people for not following the toxic psychopaths in charge. Torture, death, and public displays of terror let others know they could be next if they choose to step out of line.

On a smaller scale level in personal relationships, these same tactics are used. Sometimes it's easy to see. If you go against what they think and believe, they become monsters. Physical, mental, and emotional abuse are all consequences of anyone stepping out of line. People are either for or against them. They publicly or privately humiliate and torture those who don't follow their brainwashing.

These toxic tactics are precisely how they take us off of our guard. They amaze us with their thought processes or what they rationalize as just, fair, or rational. All of a sudden, they lose us in this sea of shock, unable to make our point. Whatever was being discussed is no longer relevant. Our minds are at a complete loss. All the energy becomes radically re-directed, as we are appalled at the whole situation. All of this energy expending achieves NOTHING and leaves our cognitive thinking skills at a complete loss.

However, there is hope for us. Start taking notes. They are shocking us with their behaviors to distract us, steal our energy, get their way, and leave us feeling powerless to their crazy-making. We can easily move beyond the technique. We are not powerless. We are powerful. We need to see the design purpose as these tactics create negative belief systems, distract us from doing things that work, and take us off guard.

Our thoughts, emotions, and energy are being played like a puppet. We need to disconnect the strings and cut the cords. As you evolve, the tactics will become transparent. You will see your old reactions to their attempts to shock and intimidate but stop playing into their hands. Instead of standing there with your mouth gaping wide open at their behaviors, unable to argue your original point effectively, you will shock them by your self-growth.

What we want to do is remove our responsibility in the equation. That requires only one person growing, changing, and becoming stronger. US. Narcissists must be wired this way so we can see what is within us fear, anxiety, powerlessness, hate, oppression, and the list could go on and on. When we stop being victims of their techniques and step up into our power, we disarm the bomb they want to engage within us.

On the small-scale personal level, the narcissist will use whatever comes close to your heart to get that emotional swing from you. This is where they find the golden honey of narcissistic supply. Empaths are big-hearted, caring, loving human beings. We are sensitive souls to the big picture world problems and abuses of society. They use our deeply empathetic nature along with something you love to shift your state of emotions, mindset, and energetic field completely.

Rememer how we talked about being an energetic outlet. Narcissists are looking to plug into us, to obtain this energy. If we think of our bodies as an electrical being composed of frequencies and vibrations emitted by certain emotions, we can further unravel the importance of the narcissist tactic. Everyone and everything is emitting an electrical field that is continually fluctuating with life situations. Here are some examples of human emotions and their frequency.

Think of this like a light bulb and its corresponding wattage.

Serenity of Being	40.0
Taking Action	20.0
Cheerfulness	3.5
Anger	1.5
Anxiety	1.05
Fear	1.0
Grief	0.5
Victim	0.1
Blame	0.03

Standing in our power unaffected by inner fears, victimization, despair, or anxieties while taking action in our lives radiates a high vibration. Exactly why self-work is so crucial to our mental, physical, emotional, and spiritual well-being. We need to be able to achieve these higher states of being regardless of what tactics are used. The narcissist is using these different loops of ups and downs like love bombing bringing us into higher states of emotions. Then shock and intimidation is utilized to drop us into lower states of emotion.

They seem like great people then pull the rug out and do some kind of mind-boggling abusive type behavior. When the narcissist shifts you from this higher state of being into fear and victimization, there is a higher output of energy to be gained. Everything we love, cherish, and hold dear to our lives is the most significant way to get that energetic feedback. With the narcissist in your life, think about how this plays out for you? They know what they can manipulate to move you into fear, anxiety, and victimization.

And it's their job to outplay our worries so we can step over them. Think about where this is happening in your life. You may notice repeat patterns where the same kind of emotional issues are targeted. Anything that is close to your heart also serves as a great tool of manipulation. Toxic people are quite cunning and instinctively know what to twist against us. Use your life and examine these different areas. How might you be playing into the narcissist techniques of shock and intimidation?

1. Children – You may worry about letting the children have visitation or what will happen if you are not around to protect the kids.
2. People close to us and our own families- They love to make big displays of drama and can often twist people against us.
3. Pets and animals- If you have issues with people who abuse animals you will be cornered into relationships with them.
4. Business relationships/Money- If you have fears around money and finances it will be the prime target.
5. Hobbies or life passions- Toxic people often end up with control of the money. They can threaten to take away your favorite hobbies or shame you.

Apply this concept to your situation and the narcissist. If you leave a narcissist, this could be a legal battle. They have some ridiculous ideas of what is their fair share. They live in a land of illusions about reality and how to split up the assets. Besides the fact they do NOT care if they blow every dollar you have in legal fees and destroy everything to the point, NO ONE gets anything.

Or it could be the children they use as pawns in their head games and hurt intentionally to make sure you pay for your choice. Maybe they have twisted lies and manipulations to make your kids turn against you. The children are afraid of going against the parent or become easily manipulated by any love bombing, so they fall into the same patterns molding and conforming to keep the peace.

On a large scale, the narcissists are using our Earth as a pawn. It's so frazzling. Why would you destroy the place you need to live? It makes no sense what-so-ever unless you understand there are two forces at work here. A set of people working to control, divide, and destroy versus a collection of people meant to heal, evolve, and protect. The nonsensible things they do have a specific role in our growth and development.

The shocking events provide them with power, control, and distract our human potential by getting us caught up in these marketed, blown out of proportion, and often fabricated dramas.

Toxic personalities love transferring people's emotional state from positive to negative vibes. They do not care if they have to twist, hurt, manipulate, or destroy everything to get this energetic feedback. Until we channel our energy into healing, evolving, and growing beyond them, the crazy-makers will dominate relationships. These patterns of manipulation carry on from one generation to the next.

A toxic child, for example, will exhibit horrific behaviors in public to get what they want. If the parent is a people-pleasing empath, they will give in to the child reinforcing bad behavior. The child learns that fit throwing and over the top displays of anger will have their parents feeding into their demands. As the child grows up, they learn how to control and manipulate by shock and intimidation. They develop relationships with people who will give into them.

What about the opposite side of the coin? An empathetic child will do everything they can and walk on eggshells to keep everyone happy. They do not like to see mom or dad ranting and raving. The narcissistic parent will choose their favorite item to use as a pawn. This makes them fearful, anxious, and uncertain. If the child does not heal and learn to overcome their fears, they will get older with these same patterns.

Then they will fall in love to find their partner uses these same techniques against them. Our families are a brilliant way the creator locks us all together into these family dynamics with people we often do not know how to deal with but cannot escape. It doesn't have to be gigantic things either. There are small ways things can happen to stir everyone up.

It could be that one person at work who is always talking about other people negatively or pushing something in your face. Your workday was going just great when they stop by to tell you how underpaid you are while the boss is just making tons of money. Maybe it's a story of how dumb the company is and what nut brained idea got pursued. You can't even get a raise, but they just paid for the top CEO's brand-new Escalades. We have to look deeper into the situation.

What if you gave up on your dreams to have the security of this job? Now, if the office narcissist stops by to tell you the drama or how underpaid you are, what happens? The inner voice that knows you chose to give up on your hidden talents and goals starts screaming. You think it's about them, but it's about you. If you are not pursuing your dreams, fulfilling your abilities, or stepping out of your fears, a nagging voice inside of you will start swirling around about the unfairness. Until we are living in the highest version of ourselves, the negative emotions won't stop.

With intimidation, it's the same story different delivery. The power the toxic personalities wield is by hitting on your fears or inability to let go. Let go of what you can't control and have faith; all things are working in perfect order. They don't threaten or twist stories randomly. It's only the areas we need to do self-work that get triggered by their tactics.

Besides, anything that you hold close to your heart threatens their position as the center of attention. Seeing people naturally happy, loving, and enjoying life gets under their skin. The relationships we have that bring us joy become their targets. They get triggered by resentment, watching something else get slathered in love. It's like they know they are not capable of this relationship and are upset on some deeper level.

Hopefully, as we all work on our issues, they will have no choice but to work on their own.

The narcissist loves to push these inner fears, anxieties, and feelings of victimization as emotional warfare to manipulate, dominate, and control us. They will threaten you with whatever treasured item may be close to you and dangle it like a carrot. How this may show up in your life may be different, but I'm giving you examples.

The underlying shock and intimidation tactics are all the same. Look for repeat patterns in relationships that emotionally trigger you. Perhaps there's a narcissist at work you need to stand up to, but you're worried you will get fired. Then how will you support your family? You feel they have some financial hold on your life. Being able to pay your bills has you locked into their crazy-making behaviors.

This triggering of FEAR inside of you is what they are meant to do. Resolve the fundamental issues, fears, anxieties, and places you are not living up to your full potential and BOOM the tactics do not work anymore. They may try to test you, but you watch the games and don't play. Living according to principles, morals, and justice would be easy if there weren't these heartstring connections.

The shocking behaviors and intimidating tactics create an illusion of control because they hit us right in our weakness. Our fears, anxieties, and inner traumas become the invisible road map they hit over and over and over again. They seek our fears and twist them against us so we can finally face them. We have our accountability in the dynamics. Perhaps you've already noticed they are not just randomly choosing targets.

Shock and intimidation can only work if we allow it to hold power over us, our actions, thoughts, emotions, and decision-making abilities. We must learn how to see through the crazy-making behaviors, identify how the narcissists are creating it, and use our weaknesses like a tool. Making a stand for ourselves when they ultimately hold some power over our lives takes faith. Faith is difficult when there is always some treasured item that we know the narcissist will try to destroy.

Another critical element that is very difficult for an Empath is letting go of trying to fix, solve, and heal everything. If the narcissist wasn't so shocking and intimidating by making these examples of their hard, cruel, and insensitive ways, we would never learn how to let go.

Let go of what we cannot fix, heal, and solve. Oh, this is a hard one! Especially when we see some horrific offenses displayed all over the news.

We want to control and dominate to create happiness, love, peace, and positive vibes. The narcissists wish to control and dominate to create some type of suffering. Guess what?

Both parties are emotionally intent on controlling and dominating, even if it is for the opposite reasons. We feel powerless, out of control, hurt and angry by our inadequacy to solve the problem. Only by letting go of other people's journeys and allowing whoever you call the creator of this world to handle the big stuff can we stop our wheel of misery.

We also have valid reasons to judge them and love on conditions. They have supplied us with all the evidence necessary to be angry, horrified, and step out of unconditional love and forgiveness. I recently saw a YouTube video of a woman named Eva Mozes Kor, a survivor of human experimentation at an Auschwitz concentration camp. She was speaking of her decision to forgive the mad scientist working for Hitler, who was responsible for continually torturing her with his experiments.

Hitler was a great example of a narcissist using shock and intimidation. The Jews were executed, tortured, and imprisoned for going against his belief systems. In the case of Eva Kor, the scientists used her as a human guinea pig in their experiments. He almost killed her, and perhaps that would have been easier than the constant torture of being injected with whatever horrific nonsense they wanted to test. Yet, here she was in this interview, clearly forgiving this human being.

She had gotten to this expanding space of forgiveness and unconditional love. There can be no more profound spiritual evolution to me than what this woman has evolved and developed.

Choosing to move beyond hating those who have displayed shocking offenses against her is amazing. She was a little girl and had done nothing wrong to deserve the treatment she received. Yet she had chosen to free herself of the experience by forgiving him. This is the only way to break the cycle.

The missing last step that many people will not ever see or obtain in their soul development. Until that happens, the cycle must continue as it's necessary for our growth. These are called spiritual tests. The toxic personalities of life have given you every possible reason to hate what will you do? Some people even though they are free from the situation can never let go of there bitterness and contempt. Unfortunately, it only hurts them and keeps the victims locked into their pain patterns.

Another necessary component is seeing the narcissist in us. The only way to see if you love on "conditions" is to have a lot of people not following the ideals. If everyone on Earth was living in peace and harmony out for the greater good, how could the love inside you be tested? Whatever our rationalization is of how things "should be" the narcissists have entirely flipped upside down. They make it so challenging to forgive and have inner peace unconditionally. The easier road is to become hurt, angry, bitter, resentful, and victimize ourselves, which is always the ego answer.

Have you watched the movie "Wonder Woman"? At the end of the show, she is being taunted to join the dark side by killing the main characters of evil. She recognizes this somewhere in the battle and realizes that they have a purpose. Every person has to decide for themselves what they will listen to within themselves. These life situations provide the perfect environment to see what is inside of us.

Just watch the news today, and you'll probably find numerous societal abuses. Besides, the news loves to twist, manipulate, and highlight everything horrific. Oh, you have a headache, it must be brain cancer. You better have a doctor check that out. They prescribe some medication that has several nasty side effects until you wish the headache was the only problem. How about the fact the only thing on the news is the worst events of the day? Where are the stories of people doing great things for others, inventing ways to stop pollution, and other amazing feats of human kind? You will never hear about them. The big scale is easy to see and very transparent, but it happens every day in small ways with the people we know.

If there is hate, guilt, shame, powerlessness, anxiety, victimization, or any kind of fear inside you, the narcissist will find and trigger it until you do the personal work to heal, evolve, and transform. The tactic of shock and intimidation will no longer trigger you when those inner issues the narcissist is bringing to light are completely resolved. Start looking at this tactic with a new set of eyeballs. Ask yourself some questions.

- What is the narcissist using to manipulate me into shock and intimidation?
- How does this fit into my fears and anxieties?
- What do I need to fix, heal, or transform within myself to overstep this hurdle and stop playing into their hands like a puppet?

This could manifest in lots of ways . . .

Example 1: The narcissist just spanked your child for not eating all of their food and is demanding they finish their plate. The plate they stacked way too much food on in the first place. What do you do? Stand up for the child or live in your fears of them and the horrible ways they shock and intimidate? Narcissists are bullies and love to make examples of people to have everyone walking on eggshells, afraid to stand up to them, and create robots.

We are cowards. We don't step up to the ring, and our higher selves know we are not living our full potential. Narcissists only target specific people, those who are weak. They never pick on someone strong enough to be a worthy opponent. I think every person in school has seen this happen. The underdog gets bullied, humiliated, and picked on. As empaths, we hate it, but don't stand up for them. We are the peacemakers, and it places us in a terrible position. Let's think about this triangle of terror in terms of the mirrors.

NARCISSISTS: Cowards who pick on the weak to mask their insecurity, wounds, and fear.

EMPATHS: Empaths who do not fully stand up for the underdog. Cowards to their inner insecurities, wounds, and fears. We must work through this issue, stand up for others, and take back our power.

VICTIM: Whatever is being picked on is mirroring their inner voice or self-abuse patterns. The emotional feed to the narcissists happens only when they hit the matching wound.

For example, I hate my big nose attracts the kid at school who runs around yelling, "your face is ugly, and you have a big nose." Self-rejection invites outside rejection. Or in the case of physical abuse, the inner voice screams a self-abuse pattern. "I don't deserve to be alive." The laws of attraction must bring in all the right people to beat you up.

It's the suffering that's a requirement to keep us looking for answers to heal. Yet none of us have been taught these concepts. We are taught to blame others rather than look deep into our soul wounds and heal the inner traumas that are creating these situations. This is a deep subject and one close to my heart. We need to start teaching our children how to heal mentally, emotionally, spiritually, and physically. If people create an over-emotional reaction in us, we should be looking inside of ourselves. Is this my insecurity and rejection of my big nose just reflecting back to me?

Once you heal your issues, traumas, and insecurities, this barrage of insults does not affect you.

The bully runs around yelling all your insecurities, and you don't emotionally react besides seeing how much you have evolved in your self-love. The victim mentality currently being taught is not working. The narcissists are not going to change. Only by each and every one of us doing our inner healing work can we change the relationship dynamics around us.

Example 2: Do you want to start your own business? You mention it to the narcissist, and here they are just whispering in your ear. "It's hard to make it." They have some horrific example of someone who lost everything when they followed their dreams. This will pound on any self-doubt you have. Like a search and destroy missionary, they know your insecurities and then voice these little seeds of self-doubt in your mind. What will you do?

None of this makes sense unless you understand the creator's design plan to expose these fears, anxieties, and inner entrapments through the illusion that we are separate. The emotional interplays between all of us are keys to where the self-work needs to be done. This illusion of shock and intimidation is another head game that appears to have life-shattering consequences. When we release all fear, negative belief systems, and re-wire our inner trauma, these systems will not work against us. The "bad" or "evil" in them is teaching us the places we haven't yet learned lessons necessary in our soul development.

Example 3: As empaths, we have huge hearts for animals. I believe they serve a very key role in these dynamics. As humans, we can wield power and control over them. Animals cannot tell on us. If you have issues with people who abuse animals, you will surely attract those who behave in shocking and atrocious ways. It's a similar storyline and lessons to the situation of bullies and cowards. One situation can teach many lessons. You cannot control everyone in this world and how they behave.

We, as empaths, have to learn to draw the line here and let go of what we can't control. Trusting the bigger picture when it looks horrific is difficult. The ego wants to scream all of the time. Everything is all wrong. Having faith that this big dysfunctional mess called Earth is just a working projection of ourselves and those unresolved issues is not easy. The more we can use these concepts, the easier it will become.

We must realize we are responsible for our karma. No matter what other people do, that is not my responsibility. The narcissist's role here is to use this big heart of yours and mistreat animals, people, whatever is dear to us right in front of you. On purpose, they want to break your heart, make you feel powerless, out of control, angry, and sad. Are these emotions sounding familiar? You are standing front and center with them mouth gaping open in wild bewilderment that anyone could be so cruel, inhumane, or unreasonable.

Or you watch the news to see some poor animal that has been terribly abused, neglected, or starved. Here you are faced with parts of yourself that you don't want to acknowledge. You can't save everything and everyone. As much as we want to control everything, we have to let go and trust the creator's design plan. Before I started to understand the design on planet Earth, this was a massive hurdle for me.

I am an animal lover. Seeing anything locked up, beaten down, starved, or neglected made me crazy. The fact I could not do anything about it made me so mad. It wasn't until I understood how karma works that I truly was able to let go. It became so clear that if you abused animals, you would reincarnate as an animal with an abusive owner. Or, if you abused children, you would come back as an animal who was forced to endure the same treatment.

Nothing on Earth is chance or coincidence. We think these things occur randomly, but they do not. A bigger picture is at play, but we have a hard time understanding and allowing others journeys to happen without our ego's judging. This would be so much easier if Earth wasn't designed with evil. Letting go of our attachments of fixing everything is not easy, but it can be done. Until you have remedied the internal soul issue it will keep attracting animal abuse to you. In some way, you will be cornered into seeing animals treated unfairly. We have to resolve the internal issues rather than try to fix other people and situations.

Ask yourself some more questions . . .

- What is the narcissist using to manipulate me by using shock and intimidation to control?
- Are the fears they are pushing onto me match where I am living in fear?
- Am I just a mess of judgments about everything and everyone all of the time?

Take the desire to judge and control everyone out of your mind the next time you watch the news, experience life with others, or find yourself in narcissistic situations. Everything here is working in its perfect order. Truly let go and embrace that everything is happening to everyone for a specific reason. When you understand the soul, all things are designed brilliantly. For every action, there is a reaction.

The second key element we must understand is the spiritual test. Life is messy. Toxic people are rude, destructive, and can be evil. They provide the spiritual test to show us where we are divided from love, being control fanatics, and can't release things to God's design. We have to love and accept ourselves being unable to fix everything. The only way to make us recognize that little beauty is to have a lot of screwed up messes going on that we have no control over. Not just in our own lives or how those around us are treated but pollution, wars, suffering, and injustice. The big agenda is to have all of us operating in ego and that black heart win. We no longer want to operate within those systems.

What are these triangles all begging us to heal? We must love ourselves in those messy moments where we cannot control the insanity of the world- the powerless, out of control, ashamed, heartbroken person who can't stop the madness happening right in front of us. Let go of what we can't fix and know God is handling the grand design. Do not let their tactics stand in our way by operating in fear, anxiety, or walking on eggshells. We are not God and could not orchestrate the world to be a perfect place. Besides, the world is working according to these universal laws. All occurrences are intertwined together to create a very cool space for us to grow and develop. What we see out there is merely the reflection of inner turmoil.

Step 1: Letting go is one of the hardest challenges, especially when you have your HEART involved. I am of God, but I am not God, and so it is not my job to figure out the "rights" and "wrongs" here. I do everything in my power to be the best I can be, no matter what happens in life. I do everything in my ability to balance, heal, and be the highest version of myself completely. The only person you can control is you. How you handle yourself, life, and other people will create suffering or happiness.

Step 2: The shocking and intimidating ways narcissists operate mirrors our ability to be ruled by their tactics. We must speak our truth, handle our fears and insecurities, and step up to the plate with the narcissist. Once you've stood up to the narcissist without fear or anxiety, having complete faith in your principles, values, and voice them, they will no longer bother you. They will be a testament to how strong you've become.

All the situations that used to have you walking on eggshells and tiptoeing around them will no longer affect you. You are standing there watching the narcissist fit throw like you would a 2-year-old who just threw themselves on the ground, flailing around, and screaming because they did not get what they want. If the parent keeps giving into this big display of drama, of course, the child keeps the behavior. Then that child keeps going back to the parent who can be manipulated.

What happens though when none of these tactics work? It's a compelling position to move into with life. Trust me. You'll be so grateful once you do. You will know without them being wired to use shock and intimidation to control you; there is no way you would have gotten this strong. We are the ones locking ourselves in their cages when we operate from our fears, anxieties, and internal traumas. Still, we have the power to set ourselves free by taking action in new directions rather than staying stuck in our repeat patterns.

All human suffering is fabricated by us, not evolving into the highest version of ourselves. Not facing our fears. Not healing our trauma. Not stepping out of victimization mentality. Finger pointing and blaming others keeps those wheels turning. Every single one of us can have a huge contribution to the current state of the world by doing that one thing, working on ourselves.

We are creating this unshakeable inner peace that is living our highest potential on Earth.

The greatest mastery you can acquire is the mastery of yourself.

CHAPTER 9
SINLESS SEXUALITY

WE HAVE JUST found out we partnered with someone who triggers, mirrors, and reflects our traumas. Then, we are supposed to have amazing, loving sexual relationships. It seems like the cruelest triangle ever designed. To admit that we have orchestrated this mess off some internal self-abuse and dysfunctional patterns is a bit mind-bending.

We are not co-sharing love in deep, meaningful ways with people who love, honor, and truly adore us. We are attracting our inner reflections, unhealed wounds, and failed spiritual tests. As the narcissists, unhealed counter-match, profound emotional issues surface and suffering. The magical connections are deeper than we see or recognize until we really start identifying our core issues. This can show up in lots of ways.

I am not enough, so being sexualized becomes a false sense of love and approval. If you find me sexy or show me some affection, it gives a temporary feeling of being loved. Look, someone is attracted to me. They like and care about me. Is it the truth? Or do they just want to use you for sex, but won't ever be there for you in ways that genuinely show loving care.

What about getting used for money, gifts, or some financial perks? You do not feel by your personality alone; someone would love or care for you. Your sexual relationship hinges on buying things for the narcissist.

No money, no relationship. The higher self or inner soul always knows the truth.

What if we are the opposite mirror? You are using someone for financial perks, money, gifts, or trips. This happens in business, marriages, and all kinds of places. Lots of self-hate can pop up. The truth is you do not believe in your gifts and talents, and this appears to be the easy way out. Perhaps you stay in a marriage with a narcissist thinking it will protect the children. Or you have been a stay at home mom for so long you don't know what you would do for a career to support everyone.

There are lots of ways to feel shame, guilt, or some repressed emotions around your sexuality. Homosexuals have heterosexual relationships to fit societal ideals. Transgender people may not be true to their feelings of who they are, so they mold and form to avoid criticism. We are not capable of allowing ourselves to be adored or loved fully.

If you are not deeply self-partnered, you will pick partners who abandon and betray you. You will attract someone who cheats, plays games, or manipulates situations. You must get secure and confident in yourself, regardless of what others do. Self-abuse patterns become crystal clear when you look at the relationship backward.

The grand high-level narcissists that make up the "powers that be" or Illuminati are pushing this dysfunctional idea of sex and sexuality at us all of the time. Sex does sell because we believe the false ideals. We are not taught to source love and approval inside of ourselves. We think someone is going to complete us.

False ideals, role models gone wrong, and dysfunctional ideas around sexuality are fed to us all of the time. We have over-complicated it with shame, guilt, pain, not good enough, and oppression. These dysfunctional running programs and faulty belief systems reflect our inner state of consciousness. I often think of the beauty of animals and how they interact with one another. There are no inner trappings of their own egos to deal with, and no one cares or looks for deep hidden meanings in their interactions.

If a female dog goes into heat, a hormonal fluctuation sends everyone into psychosis. The girls are humping her. The boys are going crazy to get over there and get it on. No one goes around talking about it, "did you see that bitch go in heat? All the other girls were trying to mount her up." None of the other dog's care or claim ownership on the male dog. "Oh, what is he doing looking at that bitch?"

In the animal kingdom, these are reproductive impulses. Nothing more. They go on, eat, sleep, have sex, and openly shit in front of each other without any feelings of guilt, shame, or internal issues. These are biological urges and processes. Yet, we are more complicated beings that love to complicate things. Plus, we have this inner desire to co-partner with the ONE perfect match.

On top of that, add a whole mess of societal belief systems, unhealed wounds, trauma bonding, and dysfunctional self-abuse patterns. You have a recipe for disaster all tangled up in these ideas of "love". We attract back to ourselves our internal working order or disorder. All souls align to show us what is going on within.

Hard wired with our sexuality as another tool to do self-work. When each of us takes back our healing and expands into our authentic selves, all of this dysfunctional mess around sexuality will disappear. To move into SACRED SEXUALITY (look for this book coming soon), we must HEAL WITHIN all of the core issues.

Achieving that level of expansion is interlaced with healing all of these other traumas. For example, if we have a negative, critical inner voice, we attract a partner who is constantly criticizing, belittling, or making some negative commentary about or to us. If we do not have love and approval of ourselves and someone negatively makes judgments of us, it cuts like a knife. Later that same person who tore us down all day wants to get romantic in the bedroom.

It's confusing for the soul. Within all of these games played, hurts being transferred, and love gone wrong we are then expected to want to make love or have sex with the person who appears to be the abuser. You may wonder, what has happened to my sex drive? Maybe it's smarter at recognizing toxic patterns than you.

This list of examples could go on and on with each person being somewhat different, but the bottom-line is the same. So where do we go from here? How do we heal unhealthy inner wounds and break free from the dysfunctional bonds? Look at some of these areas and think whether any of the categories fit into your situation.

Narcissists are very in tune with your sexual needs when they are in the love-bombing phase. They know how to please and touch you in all the right ways sexually. "Love-bombing" phases ensure some great glimpses into how beautiful the relationship could be. There's just one small problem. If you truly feel fantastic, loved, and admired, this goes beyond what they are capable of at their core. This is how they provide us with the suffering we need to see our own dysfunctions. (*You have self-abuse patterns, don't feel deserving, or cannot accept being adored. You need them to reflect the relationship you have with yourself.*)

This may not seem right because they have hooked you in with the love bombing. When they start discarding or devaluing you, it becomes painfully apparent. Narcissists play games with other people to make you jealous, criticize, shame, use, and manipulate you for their advantage. Then say, "come give me a kiss." Our internal barometers are screaming at this confusing way to "be loved" as it too is being manipulated and twisted. (*If you have weak boundaries and people pleasing issues you will let people use and abuse you, then kiss them.*)

So, you've opened up to them, and now they know what you sexually like and don't like. You are a tool under their control. They know what YOU DON'T LIKE, and they do it anyway. Or you've told them what you do like, and they don't do that on purpose. You wonder why don't they listen to me? I've told them 100 times I don't like how they are touching me, but they do it anyway. What I do enjoy they seem to NOT do on purpose unless they are "lovebombing." (*You have a hard time expressing what you need and feel in a relationship. You would rather suffer than speak up. You need to communicate clearly what you do and don't like or is not acceptable. They won't make it easy, and you will have to stand solid in your boundaries over and over and over again.)*

Maintaining long term consistently, loving relationships in a truly genuine way is not possible for a narcissist. Every element of life is twisted to get control, wield power, or make you their puppet. If you don't want sex, they want to make you have sex. If you enjoy sex, the narcissist will deny sex. They will make promises of lovemaking and then let you down. Remember, they like knowing you are on their puppet strings, just begging for a little dose of attention. Plus, there is a buildup of excitement as you think maybe I'm going to get lucky tonight. That makes the "let down" even more powerful to them when you get NO at the end of the line. (*The inadequacy within is brought to light by them. You don't feel like you deserve to be loved and adored, or you have self-sabotage programs running. You rate your worth, attractiveness, or self-esteem on whether or not you are attractive or worth it to your partner.)*

While these games are played, they will want their egos stroked. They want you to let them know that they are the best lover EVER. Remember, they are in love with themselves. We want to share love as a pure form or union between two people, and they are not capable.

(You lie to make people feel better about themselves and evade, possibly hurting someone. They must continually be looking for ego props so you can be the liar and illusionist yourself.)

Narcissists use a series of techniques to "gaslight" you about how you like sex that isn't true but fits their needs. Remember, they live in their reality that involves shifting everything for their agenda. (*If you cannot get in your body and recognize what you like and don't like, then how can you be angry with them. They must be wired to create suffering, so we will finally start paying attention to our own sexual needs.)*

Pain meaning your physical pain can be a massive turn-on for them. At a lower level, this means using all of your turns on to get you completely close to climax and then inflicting some pain to sabotage the moment. Yet, what they are doing right feels good enough in the moment to not stop them. That would be the lower level sabotage which is almost invisible until you start paying attention. Higher-level games would be S&M or some torture involved in "love." Pain and pleasure. They know exactly where to draw the line on how much you pain you will put up with for pleasure. *(Narcissists are wired to push the lines of physical enjoyment and pain in all ways. We have to match that agenda ourselves by feeling like we need to put up with amounts of pain to feel pleasure.)*

Most empaths in relationships with narcissists have issues around sex or a low sex drive, and often pick a highly sexed narcissistic partner that shame and humiliate you. For example, for men, if you have a hard time getting an erection the partner will make jokes, public remarks, or scoffs finger pointing your inability to get an erection. For a female, it would be the opposite situation where you have difficulty achieving an orgasm or are made to feel you can't satisfy your partner's needs. Really, it's completely normal to not be sexually attracted to the exact person who is underhandedly abusing you. *(This personal rating system they voice is the negative voice we have internally about ourselves, our sexuality, and our abilities to perform up to someone else's standards. We feel inadequate as we are, and they painfully often publicly announce it.)*

Highly sexed narcissists could show up in your life as entirely over-obsessed with porn, toys, gadgets, and never get enough sex. No matter what you do, they are never satisfied. They want that XXX type sex that may appall the partner who is looking to share a healthy, loving bond. They get excited over the opposite sex, make comments about their nasty thoughts, and can be quite embarrassing to you. You may know they are cheating on you, but you stay with them. For the partner of this type of narcissist, they may hurt in several ways. Why am I not good enough, and you seem to need all of these other things, porn, or partners to have a good time? Why does sex always have to be this raunchy type thing without any feelings of a deep, meaningful connection? When those comments about what they would like to do to other people or who they find attractive show-up, it makes the wounded empath feel so second rate. It is hurtful and degrading. (*I am not enough as I am is attracting you are not enough as you are, so the narcissist must seek that from someone else. Porn is also just an escape for the narcissist. The fantasy land illusion where no one has any demands or real relationships. The people don't know each other's imperfections, faults, or character flaws. It's just sexual playground that truly does not exist, a fairy tale idea they want to believe.)*

Homosexuals have another dynamic way this can manifest, although all of these factors apply to them. Sometimes, to conform to society, they find themselves trying to maintain heterosexual relationships. Or they may have some guilt, anger for the world, or negative emotion about being a homosexual. Society has decided that they are to be rejected, criticized, and outcast for their sexuality. This could manifest in a relationship by a homosexual rejecting who they are and having a heterosexual relationship. During sex, lots of emotions could bubble to the surface. They feel like they are liar and manipulator, ashamed of themselves. Here they are trapped being the things they hate in the narcissists. These emotions all create an energy feed between them and their narcissistic partner. (*Narcissists are liars and manipulators. Homosexuals having heterosexual relationships are cornered into being them. Plus, they have not deeply self-partnered and waver according to other's opinions. Living in fear of what others will think becomes a prison. They are hiding in the closet of lies and hating themselves for it.)*

Perhaps you are in a relationship with a narcissist. Still, you stay with them for any number of reasons: Financial, lifestyle, kids, business, or just plain comfortableness. You no longer love them, but there is some tie cornering you in the relationship. You have sex, even if you don't want to or regardless of your lost feelings and emotions for them. Or you fall in love with someone else. Now you've pushed yourself into another corner feeling guilty about that relationship. (*Again, just another manifestation of how we all become whores to our fears, insecurities, inner weaknesses, and lack of self-love. They use and manipulate us, but this shows us how we are using and manipulating them. Seeing our faults and guilt in operating as the narcissist is important in unconditional love, forgiveness, compassion, and peace for everyone.)*

Case Study as shared by my good friend Ginger:

As this profound unfolding of myself transpired, I realized that games were also played in the bedroom. I know you're surprised!?! What isn't a game to a narcissist? Also, I had this internal feeling about myself, reflecting every time we had sex. A whole lot of powerful emotions would affect me physically, emotionally, and energetically. I had never thought about this before I started to want to heal and evolve.

When I first started my relationship with the narcissist, everything was terrific. As time went on and different things happened in our relationship, I felt less and less attracted to him. Everything was a game of tit for tat. He was so negative about anything I wanted to do. I felt abandoned and betrayed as the phases of devaluing and discard showed up more often. I started noticing him going out of his way to help other people but arguing every time I needed something. I would wish I was those other people he was looking to impress rather than his wife.

Having children together, I began to feel locked into our relationship. I had made a commitment to them and marriage. Even if I had lost the loving sexual feelings, I would have sex when I didn't want to and when I didn't feel truly loved by him anyway. I hated myself for being in this position where I had to let someone touch me when I had lost my feelings completely. I was afraid if I didn't stay in the relationship, I would cause so much internal damage to my children.

My suffering became the lesser of the evils. Having sex was just a short entanglement to keep on keeping on and maintain relationship peace. However, it was the hardest place to escape my guilt. I truly felt like a liar, manipulator, and user. The same quality I saw in the narcissist. Here I am cornered into being "them." During intimacy, I could find no way out!

I started to study myself, my partner, and everything that was rolling through my mind during sexual encounters with one another. Interestingly enough, this took real focus as I decided that I was generally never even present mentally. My mind was escaping the experience. Too many dark emotions and self-hate got stirred up, so I just checked out. I had just gotten into a routine where I climbed on top gave a 5 to 10-minute show, orgasm, and then bamm SLEEP PLEASE!

God, I hated me so deeply in those moments. I would think, why can't I tell him no I don't want to? If I take a long shower, will he fall asleep before I get in bed? I won't have to deal with the nightly grab ass. I feel like such a whore, liar, and manipulator. I'm just avoiding the truth because it's so painful, and it affects so many people. I trapped myself into the whole screwed up mess and I am feeling so many deep dark emotions. I started trying to recognize what was coming up for me when he would touch me.

ASHAMED

POWERLESS

GUILTY

ANGRY

FRUSTRATED

OUT OF CONTROL

What if I came clean here and told the truth? There isn't a way out of this that doesn't involve hurting people. I would worry about our kids, and he would taint them against me. There would be no concern for their emotional well-being or if he destroyed them in the process. And that's when the self-pep talk would start as I knew this was the lesser of the evils. Come on, let's get this over. Climb on and ride the devil lol!

That was the epiphany moment. I don't want to be that girl. I want to be the powerful woman who says NO I'm not in the mood. God, would I ever get in the mood with him? I don't know, who cares. What matters is I have rejected this part of myself for so long. I don't love me as I am. I wonder if he would want me so much if I stopped this circus of self-hatred when we had sex? I mean, is it the sex or the fact it's just another tool to manipulate where I feel bad about myself?

Does it matter? My body is just a way for me to work out my inner traumas. What if I loved and accepted me just the way I feel when we have sex? Whatever feeling I am having, I'll just let is show up and deeply love myself in that space. For so long, I've repressed those emotions and avoided connecting to my feelings. I started looking at my thoughts and where I hated myself. I couldn't escape my internal truths.

I am a liar and a manipulator.

I am a whore for my children and our lifestyle.

I am ashamed of who I am when we have sex.

I feel so angry and powerless in this situation.

I really can genuinely embrace this dark side of myself in love in those moments. My orgasms became releasing all of that anger and resentment I had been holding inside for YEARS. I started letting go, and sex became deeply healing. I started listening to my emotions, thoughts, and feelings, allowing them to surface whereas before I just tried to blank out. My self-hatred and self-rejection were so intense I mentally and emotionally checked out. As I geared up towards climax, I would visualize all of these negative emotions released in the orgasm.

I even turned my inner thoughts into a rambling of finally allowing myself to feel. I stopped repressing everything and went into it deeply. Right while I was getting triggered by allowing him to touch me, that's what needed to happen. I wanted to face me finally — the imperfect, broken part of my soul full of faults, imperfections, and wounds.

"I've been so mad at myself for so long for having sex when I don't want to. I feel so powerless and ashamed. I hate myself for not standing up for ME. I hate myself for just giving into your demands. I feel like I have no control over my life. What if I just decided to love myself right now exactly as I am? The powerless me, the out of control me, the doormat me, the ashamed me, the liar and manipulator, the user."

As I started coming closer and closer to my orgasm, I built all of this energy up. I visualized pulling all the negative emotions from every space, every cell, and every darkest corner of my being. This silent self-talk became my best friend. "I've been holding onto these feelings for so long. What if I decided to let this anger go? What if I just released it right here, right now, through this orgasm? I'm so ready to let it all go." When I hit that orgasm, I visualized every bit of anger released through that real physical experience. All those negative feelings I HAD FOR ME I released into the climax and watched disappear into smoke.

As the waves of the orgasm sent those feelings of temporary ecstasy over me, I envisioned them as being unconditional love filling up my entire being. Sex became my great transformer! I visualized all of these light rays filled with unconditional love, forgiveness, bliss, and peace, running through my veins to every cell every microparticle.

This LOVE is for YOU EXACTLY AS
YOU ARE whatever that may be…

HAVING SEX WHEN YOU DON'T WANT TO

SELF-HATE

ASHAMED

POWERLESS

ANGRY

HURT

DEPRESSED

OUT OF CONTROL

BITTER

Think about your sexual relationships and get real with yourself… truly down and dirty. That way, you have a complete expulsion of the negative feelings for YOU! The physical orgasm becomes a pushing out of dark energy and a pulling in of light energy. When those orgasmic waves wash over you release every negative emotion inside of you that you have connected to sex, yourself, and your relationship. See, feel, imagine, and use whatever technique seems to resonate with you as a tool. Every part of the incoming feeling is unconditional love, forgiveness, gratitude, peace, joy, and bliss.

You could be in the opposite situation. They enjoy building you up, giving you hope, and then denying you sex. You are running the negative state by some division of love inside yourself. What thoughts run through your head when they turn you down? Rejected, betrayed, abandoned, unloved, not worth it,...

That's the key to finding a resolution here. Ask yourself questions. What is your relationship with sex reflecting about your unhealed trauma within you? YOU are the lock and key! Anywhere you are divided from love for yourself will keep showing up in your life. We need to be clear on discovering all of these elements.

Do you see you picked someone who made you feel powerless, ashamed, and angry surrounding sex so you could finally heal this inner-wound? You attracted the perfect person to mirror those internal feelings and exactly where you divided from LOVE for YOURSELF. You just never understood how to see through the misery. Who knows how long you've been carrying these unhealed wounds?

If you don't resolve whatever pattern shows up, it will repeat with a new partner. The only way to heal is to love yourself in those messy and dysfunctional ways you don't want to accept. You don't want to see, feel, or acknowledge the raw, real, exposed you. If your partner doesn't want you or makes excuses to not have sex with you, the responsibility is yours. You internally don't feel you deserve to be adored or loved. That is what our sexual partners bring to light. The dysfunctional running programs run our show and create these "attractions." The energetic bonds hook us into one another.

You will also find out something profound. When you heal all of the issues that the narcissist is triggering, you will find a natural return of the loving attraction. You break the bonds with dysfunctional love and sex. That requires doing the self-work and putting it into action. Our internal crossed wires must match their crossed wires. When we do the re-wiring and heal, the attraction dies.

Let's examine one more case study to expand on this little gem:

Roger had been married to her wife, Sally, for ten years. He finds some information on narcissists and controlling personalities. Wow! A lot of things start connecting here. Roger starts to notice a lot of things. There seemed to be this whole commentary around their sex life in public.

Over time he has found he lost his ability to get an erection. It is so embarrassing not to be able to "get it up." Sally was sexually driven and made constant complaints. "Roger, can't get it up." Or some joke would be made revolving around his inadequacies in the manhood department. It was so frustrating to him. He was already so angry with himself and didn't need her publicly hammering him on it?!?

This is what narcissists do and why they are wired to be inconsiderate, "jerks" who love picking on every internal weakness. The shame they are always throwing at us is looking to find our internal match. Is this somewhere you feel ashamed of yourself? You are angry with yourself and feeling inadequate. That's where the energy is and why we need them to create the suffering, so we will finally face it and heal.

Roger is carrying self-anger, guilt, and feelings of inadequacy for his inability to get an erection. His wife is merely doing her job of humiliating him in public or private, so he can finally unconditionally love and accept himself. Every time her remarks come up, he shifts his energy into self-anger, disappointment, powerlessness, and whatever else may show up for him emotionally. Being an empath, he of course just sits and takes it without anyone ever knowing his feelings. The narcissist dramatizing any issue matches his desire to minimize everything. But the shift in his energy field is the real truth. Roger has invisibly shifted into negative emotions and feelings.

He will be in this same pattern over and over until he decides to do the inner work. It is more than just sexual. That's only the method to trap us into the dynamics. Think about all the concepts we have been learning. Does Roger have erectile dysfunction?

No, he has self-abuse patterns. He partnered with someone who emotionally and mentally beats him up all day. It makes sense for the physical part of his body to not be able to get aroused. Figure out what is happening emotionally in your body thinking about all the elements we have discussed. Release all the negative trauma and firmly ground in unconditional love. Be honest without beating yourself up. What is reflecting here that needs to heal?

If Roger gets down to the basis of his relationship, he will see precisely why he cannot get an erection anymore. He most likely also has low testosterone levels. The female narcissists have the power and control unless he heals these inner wounds and takes back his personal power and control. She has his balls in a vice grip literally and physically. Until then, he must lock into relationships that create a lot of negative emotions. The women have the power and control.

It is all wrong, yet we do not know how, why, or what to do about it?!?

Now you have the keys. You must work on yourself to change the soul mate attractions. If you stay in the fantasy land of being a victim, nothing will change. The same type of partners will keep showing up. True healing can only occur when you do all the self-work, they are mirroring back to us. You came into this place carrying this load of internal issues that get projected onto the screen set we call "life, relationships, and LOVE." These dark souls are here to show you what desperately needs to heal.

Perhaps it shows up with a child molester when you are growing up, but now you are an adult. You have chosen to marry your soul mate, yet you find you are still having sex when you don't want to.

Or you marry the abusive spouse. You no longer love them but force yourself to have sex to keep things together for the children.

Maybe you're a homosexual maintaining a heterosexual relationship.

Maybe you feel trapped in a relationship with a narcissist but fall in love with someone else.

Maybe you have a switched internal link that means being sexualized is a source of love and approval.

Perhaps it's just a way of survival as you trade sex for your lifestyle, money, or gifts.

Or the opposite, you are trading money, gifts, and trips for sexual experiences.

The underlying feelings are the same; only the situations vary.

There are lots of ways for that anger around yourself, those weaknesses, and sex to manifest, making them reflect in the exterior world. All these paths may look very different, but the bottom-line emotions all run the same. You attracted each situation as a messenger to expose the unhealed wounds. You used to believe everything is about "them." Now you know everything is about "you."

What is this for you? If you genuinely stop pointing the finger and look at yourself, what's there reflecting? The most significant shift you need to make in all elements of the narcissist relationship is looking into every situation backward. How are the narcissist's qualities showing me what I need to heal? If they are a mirror image sending me messages to my internal compass, what is it saying?

The elements of feeling "chemistry" with someone are the basis of a simple yet complicated design system. This is why we are not as simple as animals in our sexual interactions and must desire long-lasting relationships with the ONE. Yet, you can only experience sex with someone as deeply as you have met yourself. Your body, on an energetic level, is broadcasting these fears, judgments, and self-abuse patterns. The internal work must be completed for the external world to shift our relationship dynamics.

Once we move through these internal working disorders, you can broadcast new levels of intimacy because you have decided to become intimate with profoundly knowing and healing yourself. Only then can the healthy, sexual relationship come into your life. Most people call these partners the twin flame. More on this in a future book, "Twin Flame Truths".

Regardless when you achieve this level of wholeness, you are complete within yourself. All of these imbalances, imperfections, inner trauma's, and self-abuse patterns have been addressed, balanced, and healed. Only then do you break the energetic interlockings between an you and narcissists. Without getting too complicated, I will say this. A whole new level of sexual relationships will happen as more and more people evolve themselves. We are in a fascinating period of evolution!

CHAPTER 10
ROCK SOLID

I CAN'T WAIT for you to see what happens when you get rock solid in yourself. Healing, evolving, up-leveling, and sealing these wounded elements of your soul will allow you to stop hooking into what we once considered the narcissists naughty behaviors. There's a profound shift that happens. They no longer see you as a valuable source of energetic supply, material resources, social status, or however, this shows up. The game set up rolls on, but now you are awake and do not play with them anymore.

All the inner wounds they used to trigger are healed. You are no longer angry with them but grateful for the growth you can clearly see. What a powerful experience! You work with any personality utterly unaffected by their behaviors. Your outlook on them has changed completely. They have been giving us a great gift — the keys to doing our healing, balancing, and soul work. How very exciting for us to be at this point of development as we've worked through these imbalances, dysfunctional wheels, and failed spiritual tests.

The narcissist was such a priceless messenger. You are really solid in yourself and authentically who you are at the core. If they were not exactly how they are, you would never reach this inner strength. When you genuinely get rock solid in your raw, authentic self, you will handle them with ease.

I know if you're beginning your journey, this may sound way out there! I remember being curled in a ball crying about the narcissist. Begging and pleading for God to pave my way out. Yet, there I was stuck and forced into the corner with the "enemy." What I deeply realized was the enemy wasn't out there. It was within myself. Being in relationships with narcissists triggered me into those places.

Do you know what else these personality types made me realize?

How much I loved based on conditions just like the narcissist. I wanted everyone here and the world itself to mold to me so I wouldn't have to stand up for myself. Let's remove bossy, controlling, negative personalities, so I don't have to face the fact I don't voice my opinion. I'm non-confrontational. I'm a pushover. I'm gullible. Unconditional love doesn't have this set of standards that certain people need to be exterminated to get rid of the problem.

This old mindset of mine is what creates fights and divisions between us. Precisely what the narcissist so desperately wants from us. What if there is no right or wrong just a whole bunch of people operating off these unhealed wounds, failed spiritual tests, dysfunctional running programs, and inner pain? How these wheels work and turn together is completely necessary for each person to reflect those healed or unhealed wounds on the other person.

Maintaining a constant state of unconditional love is an essential part of what we are learning here on Earth. Narcissists want to control everything to feed themselves with money, power, resources, and energy. Empaths want to control everything to heal, unify, and live in harmonic peace. The opposing forces are triggering the control fanatic on both sides. Control is always ego. If it weren't for them wanting to destroy everything with their crazy-making behaviors, the healers would not be pushed into ego themselves or seeing their weak areas.

Nor would there be consequences for us all sitting around handing over our power. The more we can do this personal work, the more we can shift the paradigms on an individual and global level. Soul pollution is mirrored back with environmental pollution. Toxic relationships with ourselves reflect our toxic relationship with Mother Earth. Other people and our reactions to them are like looking into a prism.

Reflections!

Self-realization is full of great "a-ha" moments. You see, you are both the narcissist and the empath. This is so important. Seeing our inner beast releases us from judgments, negative emotions, and anger. I realize the empath and narcissist both have different agendas. Still, our guilt is undeniable. The techniques, tools, and tactics of the narcissist are necessary to strengthen us where we are weak.

They play such an important and necessary role in our development if we can see the purpose and design elements. We can all change a compelling dynamic between us, using these concepts. The narcissist becomes the stepping stone to get stronger, see our weaknesses, become more balanced, and jump these spiritual hurdles.

- ***Love bombing or Idolize:*** The narcissist on purpose knows how to be the exact perfect "soulmate" and showers us with love, attention, and affection. Our egos love this phase. It means we don't have to deal with our faults, imperfections, and weaknesses. This state of illusions, fantasy land, fairy tale type love lures us into the palm of their hands. We also have not become the source of love, approval, and support to ourselves. That makes the narcissist have control of "love". We base our fractured self on their gifts, sweet loving messages, and charming acts which many times involve public displays of profound adoration. Our egos become hooked into this phase even though it is not real, authentic, or an honest relationship. They put on the dreamy illusion, and we want to believe it. *Spiritual growth: Accept our guilt in wanting to live in the land of illusions. Recognize how the fractured parts of yourself used to be reliant on this phase to gain your sense of love and approval. Understand that there is no reason to feel guilty. The person* *you decided to put your faith and trust in was very believable and painted a beautiful picture of the future together. Besides, we need this phase, so we will sign up for the self-development program that comes from this personality type.*

- ***De-value:*** You will find this is the real heart and soul of your relationship where all of your insecurities, weaknesses, and dysfunctional running programs come to light. We have gotten used to the fairytale. Now they have pulled the rug out from under us. We, on our own free will, have chosen to sign up with their program because the "love bombing" feels so good. We have become completely absorbed into the narcissist, but what is happening now?!? They are criticizing, disapproving, and no longer attentive to us. Where is our drug???? This becomes entirely uncomfortable for us at a soul level. We want and need everyone to be happy, loving, and peaceful. Our old wounded self would be spinning circles trying to give the narcissist whatever they need to return to the love bombing. Like drug addicts, the old patterns would be turning around and around. Now we see that where the emotional reactions occur is the key to our internal issues.

  We know what to do! Do the criticisms match our inner voice? Did we become dependent on them to give us love and approval that we do not have inside of ourselves? When they stop the "love bombing," we step up to the plate and finally become a source of love, support, and approval of ourselves. Do we need to get our friends, hobbies, and passions, so we no longer have this co-dependent relationship? Perhaps it's financial. The narcissist looked like they were so great at handling money and would be giving. We have signed over control of ours. Now we are getting shamed and gaslighted about what we spend while they spend all of the money on themselves. Is it reflecting our inability to receive? *Spiritual growth: We have to take our power back. Heal any reflecting inner dysfunctional running programs. Look at what they criticize, critique, and shame you for to see if it's merely where you criticize, critique, and shame yourself. Use any tactic to soul inves-*

tigate, heal, evolve, and resolve your inner conflicts. Honestly, when we are our sense of support to ourselves, the de-value phase does not affect us beyond seeing it as a measurement of our growth.

- ***Discard:*** At one time, you idolized them because they swept you off your feet. You handed them power over your life. Now you see the ways they lured you in and exactly why it was necessary. When others discard us, it is only painful if we have these matching inner wounds. Are you now being completely ignored? Do you completely ignore your own needs? Someone else is getting the «love bombing,» and the narcissist has pushed them right in front of us. How are they using other people to make us feel jealous and insecure? Yet the insecurity, not good enough, and all of those old programs cannot get triggered when you reach real self-confidence not wavered by the actions of others. You have deeply self-partnered now. No matter who abandons and betrays you, it does not affect you. Lots of soul lessons are learned as you realize you are your source of love and approval!

  All the sudden, you are independent of them and the cycle of abuse. You no longer get "hooked in" because it has taught you what you needed to know. What was once a series of traumatic ups and downs, along with their behaviors, is just a reminder of how far you've come on your soul healing evolution. You see the value they have added in your life by painfully pointing out those imbalances, insecurities, and weaknesses. When you fully evolve if the narcissist breaks away, throws a new lover in your face, or uses any of their tactics to reject you, it does not affect you whatso-ever. *Spiritual growth: You see the outside treatment of others as a mirror into your wounded parts. Isn't it time you decided no matter who abandon and betrays you, you will always be a source of love and approval to yourself? You are no longer on anyone's puppet strings. Now if the narcissist discards you the only emotional reaction you will have is the knowledge you have healed and grown beyond them. The trauma bonding no longer exists.*

- ***No Response:*** Have you ever tried to make a plan with a narcissist? Whooooooaaaa! It›s completely impossible, and before we would have gotten frustrated and angry. How does the narcissist know what they will feel like doing that day or what they will want to do? Everyone should be like a puppet on their strings. The unhealed co-dependent version of us used to sit and wait for their answer. Now we make our plan! If they show up great and if they don't, they knew what was happening. If it's unavoidable that our plans hinge on them and their mood swings, we don't get worked up. We are trusting the universal order of things to line up scheduling for the highest good. The unaccountability in them is working out the control fanatic in us, hahaha. We are learning where to hold on and where to let go. They are great teachers to us by being impossible to form a solid plan. *Spiritual growth: Letting go and allowing the universal order to work everything out. Make your plans. Do not rely on waiting for anyone else to do anything. We try to arrange, schedule, and inform the narcissist. Then let whatever falls into place work out. If there is no response or they cannot make it, we move on with our plans unaffected by them.*

- ***Gaslighting:*** The narcissist used to win at every hand because they would lie and manipulate situations, people, and events to convince you they are right. Before you questioned and doubted yourself, but now you are questioning and challenging them. You have also decided to check in on life rather than floating, daydreaming, and not being fully present. The personal attacks no longer hold any value as valid. «You›re crazy. That never happened.» You know their twisted game and stand solid in your opinion without doubting yourself. *Spiritual growth: Believing, trusting, and standing up for your gut feeling and intuition. You are now fully present and paying attention. You are no longer skeptical of yourself but suspicious of them.*
  YouTube Video Link: Gaslighting Revelations
- ***Liar and Manipulator:*** The days of being gullible and naïve to people are over. You start watching people's actions before you develop trust in them. You are educated in how the universe,

you, and others operate so you can untangle the web. What is behind this person's motivation? Where do stories, actions, and energy not all line-up? You are wary of the constant victim stories now. Empaths will trip over themselves to never say anything wrong about anyone, while narcissists twist and taint our naïve perspectives. When they try to sell you that shiny apple, you do your homework before you take a bite. You have learned as the giving tree that not all people deserve your trust, time, energy, and attention. *Spiritual growth: Pay attention to people's behaviors and actions alone to discover how they line up with the truth. Words are easy to say, and people use them freely. Actions are much more accountable. Besides, now that you're educated on "love bombing." You realize all that glitters is not gold. Learning who to trust, when, and about what is critical.*

- ***Confrontational:*** Awe, remember the days when their temper tantrum and fit throwing made you want to be invisible. They were the ticking time bomb that you never knew how to dismantle. Now you›ve entered the ring and no longer walk on eggshells for them. You are trained and highly skilled at all their angles of attack. Where you once felt weak and powerless becomes a stepping stone to feeling powerful, assertive, and in control. The only peace there is on this Earth is created on the inside by speaking your truth, standing for yourself calmly, in power, and not being wavered emotionally by anyone›s temper tantrums. *Spiritual growth: Remaining calm under all circumstances. You are in an argument with someone trained in all your hot spots and weaknesses. Now that you've used all those emotional triggers to heal, they don't work you up in the same way. Self-Control develops and is strengthened as you create, maintain, and operate in harmony while dealing with conflict.*
- ***Triangulation:*** Every time the narcissist tries to use a gang of their brainwashed comrades, it no longer bears any effect on you. You are so strong in who you are, what you think, and your own opinions. It doesn't matter if he/she says God is on their side,

and religious narcissists absolutely will do this. You know the tools of manipulation oh so well and do not fall prey. Plus, you've developed healthy triangles with genuinely supportive and loving people. These people know and understand what you are dealing with and provide a network of love and compassion. *Spiritual growth: Knowing within yourself your viewpoints, who you are, and what you stand for regardless of who stands with you. Even if you're attacked by a liar and manipulator and their tribe, you do not waver.*

- ***Hoovering:*** When you get your friends and interests, the narcissist feels threatened. They want you to focus, rely, and depend on them. Before you revolved yourself on being available to them, let›s face it, they were your love-bombing drug dealer. Now you are completely balanced, and the hoovering does not work as much as they may try. You do not bend and flex to their every demand or have to be completely absorbed in them while they are around. *Spiritual growth: Movement from co-dependent to independent.*
  YouTube Video Link: Hoovering
- ***Projection:*** Wow! Understanding projection is such a cool tool to let go of a lot of confusion, pent up anger, and frazzling moments. Now you understand that much of what the narcissist points the finger about is their guilt. You have been gullible to their tactics because you projected your good qualities on them while they project their bad qualities on you and others. You know how to ask yourself the appropriate questions to dismantle who is projecting what where. Seeing your issues separate from theirs makes it easy to let go of their criticisms. The days of allowing them to hand over their blame to you are over. You also recognize they are not capable of being accountable. There is no reason to waste energy by making them see your point. *Spiritual growth: You can fully separate whose issues are whose. They cannot see their faults, and you move from a place of misunderstanding to compassion. You see your role in this dynamic. You were the reflection as all you saw were your faults. Now you can separate the two. You no longer take the blame for other people's issues. You accept accountability for yours*

without anxiety or trauma. This takes complete awareness of ourselves and others, without letting ego stand in our way.

- ***Blanket generalizations/Re-routing:*** We used to get lost in the narcissist›s eloquent ability to redirect the conversation, talk in circles, attack our imperfections, and make general claims with no supporting details. When you are in a disagreement, you no longer follow their lead. You continually lead them back to the original issue. They try all the tactics, but you know what they are doing in attempting to avoid their guilt. Besides, you see the experience as a key to your soul map. Will they trigger you with old wounds, unresolved trauma, past imperfections, and insecurities? Narcissists know anywhere there is shame, guilt, or blame still left inside of you. That's precisely where they redirect the conversation. Somewhere you were in the wrong or are holding self-judgments. You get emotionally triggered, shaken, and thrown off guard. Your initial point never gets addressed. Now that you've faced all those elements of yourself, you are in control and command. Before you left feeling like the original point you wanted to discuss was never even addressed. You became the object of attack, but now you are standing in your power. They can't escape your tactics as you keep moving the conversation back to the original issue. *Spiritual growth: We are not dominating or being dominated. We have become calm, perfect expressions of authentic truth. You maintain the subject at hand, as well as your point. You no longer get distracted by their tactics, like a dog chasing its tail.*
- ***Unrealistic Expectations:*** Remember that internal trauma «I›m not enough» or those weak boundaries we used to have. Before they matched the narcissist as they are the never satisfied taskmaster. You accomplish something and then they move the goal post. Now you are no longer running those programs. You can see how the narcissist's unrealistic ideals were spurring this inner wound. They are never going to be happy with you, as you were never satisfied with you. You stop asking, "how high" when they say "jump." You don't take it personal when you cannot make

their constant demands. You see how weak your boundaries were before. They pushed more than was humanly possible on your plate and then made you feel less than when you couldn't perform up to their standards. No one can make us feel "less than" unless we internally feel it within ourselves. You start saying no and setting realistic ideals, goals, and commitments. When they don't validate your contribution, you validate your contribution. When they pick at that one fault to magnify your weakness's you unconditionally love yourself and your imperfections. You are no longer playing into their games to extract energy, time, and resources from you. You set your realistic expectations, expect full payment for your time and energy, plus can say no crushing the people pleaser inside of you. *Spiritual growth: I am not enough as I am, becomes I am enough. You stop having unrealistic expectations of perfection from yourself. Self-Anger, disappointment, and your unrealistic expectations of yourself are now realistic about what is humanly possible. Self-Approval, setting practical ideals, and standing for them is your new working motto.*

- ***Smear Campaigns:*** The grand actor is up to their tricks by using others against you. They have portrayed themselves as the innocent victim. You are the abuser, toxic person, and dysfunctional part of the relationship. It can be so challenging when you know lies have been twisted against you. Before, this would have frustrated you to no end. Both wounded empaths and narcissists are people pleasers and worry about what others think of us. Now you realize you have to know who you are, what you stand for, and your principles to gain inner strength. No matter what anyone else thinks or who falls prey to their charms and manipulations, you stand firm in yourself, your values, principles, and know the truth. This is an invaluable experience to gain inner solidity and be un-wavered by other's opinions. *Spiritual growth: Insecure to the opinions and criticisms has evolved to secure and confident despite how others see you. You would not develop this without these per-*

sonality types smearing your name, twisting lies against you, and manipulating situations to make others have false opinions of you.

- ***Dominate/Control:*** They love having power over you, and in the past, you have given yours away. Yet, you have to have an active role in this by being dominated and controlled. Anger, frustration, self-doubt, insecurity, powerlessness, and anywhere you feel negative emotions is about you handing them your power. You are no longer a yo-yo or a puppet on their string, or should I say you are no longer a prisoner to your fear, self-doubt, insecurities, and weaknesses. Now you see crystal clear how to respond in an evolved way. You›re dominating and controlling yourself, your emotions, and your life. You don›t let them pull your puppet strings anymore. This means taking back your financial life, decision making, setting boundaries, and escaping the brainwashing. *Spiritual growth: We are no longer moldable and bendable to others' demands. People may want to dominate and control us, but we do not allow it. We are in control of our lives and step into our personal power.*
- ***Destructive Conditioning:*** Anything you love or found enjoyment from before the narcissist took control is re-introduced into your life. You find joy in your hobbies, holidays, and all life events no longer revolve around the narcissist. Your inner talents resurface. You are constructively re-conditioning yourself. The narcissist hasn›t been able to stand your happiness. They manipulate everything that does not revolve around them to be connected to trauma by their sneaky set of tactics. Frustrating you, sabotaging any fun, throwing temper tantrums, playing the victim, and all their little games become obvious. Nothing stands between your goals, friends, interests, and family fun plans. You have disconnected the cord that led from you to their reactions. *Spiritual test: You have learned exactly where to no longer hook into the narcissist. You choose your constructive voice regardless of them and their reactions. No one can sabotage our happiness unless we allow it. Victim moves to Empowered.*

YouTube Video Link: Narcissist Steals Joy

- ***Abandonment and Betrayal:*** The narcissist is completely wired to be unable to commit to one person in a balanced, loyal, loving relationship on purpose. They need to get attention from lots of different people, jobs, life situations for a soul purpose in our development. We have not yet deeply self-partnered, becoming a source of love, approval, and support of ourselves regardless of what others do or needing it from anyone else. While you are together, the narcissist uses games between all of these "fan club" members to gain attention, validation, and their ego props. You're jealous of the entourage. The entourage is jealous of you. This creates a lot of energetic triangles, with the narcissists being the center focus. Now you use this as an opportunity to gain self-confidence and self-reliance. You can see the mirror is exposed. The narcissist is insecure, so they must have many admirers. The empath is insecure, so they feel like this must be a symbol that they are not enough. The wounds match until the empath no longer wavers their self-love, approval, or support according to what anyone else does or does not do. Once you unhook entirely with the narcissist as some type of commodity, they may decide you are no longer worth the energy they are expending. The unhealed parts no longer match up. They love to bounce between makeup and break up, but this may lead to the final break up. If you have not learned everything, you need to know or healed the trauma bonds. It will be painful. You will take this personal. If you have deeply healed, you will find a whole new response within yourself. When they pull the plug on you, you don't take it to heart. You realize that you projected your ideas of a relationship on the love-bombing illusion. The new partner they are idolizing at the moment is a mirror into your former unhealed self and only a tool to them. The deep wounding of being abandoned and betrayed does not happen as you recognize this as an epic statement of your development and healing. Now you are free to enter a relationship that mirrors the deeply self-partnered, expanded, balanced, healed version of you. *Spiritual Growth: A deeper, more compassionate heart emerges for the narcissist and their new partner. You see how the relationship was a stepping stone and balancing point for your growth. The feelings of being abandoned and betrayed no longer exist. Your self-love and commitment to love, honor, and cherish yourself is not impacted by what others do or don't do. This is the space for the new, up-leveled, healed version of yourself to be mirrored back in a new partner.*

Here are a few essential tips to remember when dealing with narcissists, toxic, controlling, and manipulative personalities:

1. When having a different opinion, do not be wavered on what you think and feel. Be aware your job is to state your thoughts, belief systems, or ideals but then be unattached to their reaction. They love arguments, drama, and find it particularly fun if you get emotionally wrapped up in trying to make your point be heard, acknowledged, and accepted. If the narcissist is not capable of recognizing your point of view, agree to disagree. It's not about them honoring your opinion. What you are begging yourself to do is be heard by YOU! Regardless of what anyone believes, does, or thinks I am valid and have a right to be heard. Do not let your voice be squashed, but do not try to convince them of anything. You do not have to agree to respect each other's opinions or love one another. Understand you can control your reactions and how you deal with people. THAT'S IT! Everyone else is merely living their life according to their viewpoints, unhealed traumas, karmic journeys, and reality. In terms of the narcissist, this may be nowhere near your truth. That serves a powerful lesson. We do not all have to agree to get along and love one another.
2. Love yourself exactly as you are; however, you are warts and imperfections. They will want to manipulate those against you. Anytime you feel bad about yourself address the unhealed wound or imbalance they triggered. They are doing their part to painfully

point it out. Don't let them break your "bliss bubble," and the stronger you get, the harder they try.

3. Regain relationships with people that are HEALTHY and SUPPORTIVE. Do not expect that relationship between them. Do be prepared for them to try to shred those relationships up! They will want to drive a wedge between you and loved ones by fit throwing, the silent treatment, or blow-ups. You have to stop letting them pull you into their emotional wheel. It's up to you. Do not get angry with them about their selfishness either. They are making you stand up for your boundaries and get stronger. Be grateful that's a weakness inside you, and this is your change to step up for yourself. Feel compassionate for them. Sadly, they are not capable of maintaining healthy relationships.
4. Every time they do not validate you... VALIDATE YOURSELF! They on purpose, are not going to give you credit for your accomplishments or be happy for your success. They find it intimidating to their ego. You will have to become that sense of support, love, and validation to yourself. The happier you become, the more it will push their buttons to tear you down. That's just testing you! Are you still emotionally on their puppet strings?
5. Set your boundaries. Know exactly what you will and won't do. This can be the hardest part for empaths. We are giving trees, and that's why they saw us as a commodity. The reason covert narcissists are so good at luring us into their trap is because they speak directly to our egos. That is why "love-bombing" works... Oh, you are so perfect and wonderful, followed by something they want you to do for them. Or the infamous draw of them being so attentive, charming, and sparkly after mistreating or using you. You just worked 100 hours of overtime unpaid without their help on a big project, and now that it's the final moments of completion, they showed up with a "gift" and are here to help. You have to draw the line for yourself and FIGHT for it regardless of the "love bombing". Here you are non-confrontational and a constant giver. Decide to set limits even though they are very good at all

their tactics. You can only be affected by the silent treatment, shaming, or gaslighting if you allow it to bother you. If it's still bothering you there are more imbalances, mirrors, or wounded parts that need to heal. In the end you will be fully capable of setting your own rules and standing for them despite the narcissist's storms. You can do it!

6. If you are battling for something you feel is right, be prepared to lay out the red carpet as to how this decision or agreement will BENEFIT the narcissist. They are egomaniacs, so you can also use sheltering their public appearance as an essential cornerstone. Add in some little comments, "How will it look to everyone if you don't support ___________?" They are masters at triangulation, meaning using an outside person to corner or gaslight you. Remember, they like triangles, so don't be afraid to use them. For example, if they are flirting with someone and you call them out on it, you will be disregarded and de-valued. As soon as you add in another person, they know you trust the ears may open to your comment. This is more powerful. For example, my mom noticed she was hanging all over you. She asked me if something was going on between you two! Ut oh!! You've just messed with the narcissist's false image here. They want to keep that in check. Know their hot buttons and how to stand for yourself.
7. Get ready to move through the co-dependent part of you. Get at peace with relying on your skills, intuition, and abilities. One reason the narcissists must be wired to not be there for us is so we can work through this inner issue. If there is any way you are hiding behind them, it will surface within the relationship. It pushes you to step up to the plate. Get serious with yourself. Where am I getting my self-love from someone else? How am I hiding behind them, and the fact they have left me high and dry is forcing me to work this fundamental issue out? Have I given up my goals and dreams to revolve around them and need to pursue them again?
8. Ask yourself, are you the "needs to be needed" attracting the "needy"? The narcissist knows how to feed your ego and make

you feel "special" during the love bombing phases. What if you didn't have that feedback anymore? If you removed all the plugs on all the kind comments, others made about you as a person what then? Or do you need to be validated by someone else to fill up that empty love tank inside? Not that helping each other isn't important, but only when it's in balance.

9. Get to know who you are without anyone else's opinions. The narcissist is a fake, but so are every single one of us. Society, our parents, belief systems, all kinds of elements have been shaping you since you were young. Strip away all of that and figure out who you are at your core. Do you have natural talents that you stopped pursuing because your self-doubt, insecurities, and dysfunctional wounds are running your life? Are their things you enjoy the narcissist destroyed? It's time for a soul resurrection.

10. Give validation to the narcissist. There is nothing wrong with admiring the narcissist's strengths. They can also be great people in lots of ways. When you start healing yourself, and their tactics no longer work, it's so much easier to enjoy their company. We think we are angry with them. Doing self-work shows us we are attracting our matching unbalanced counterparts. I have learned a lot from narcissists not because the relationship was easy, but because it forced me to work on myself and kept creating suffering because of my "bad" qualities. We all have good and bad qualities, and narcissists are not the enemy. Besides being great athletes, master manifesters, skilled professionals, leaders, and go-getters are qualities I admire. Every person here has something to teach us, and continually working on ourselves is the actual task.

11. Be aware they are not here to help you in the traditional sense. Narcissists will sabotage your happiness and success on purpose. If you start a diet, they will push some sweet treat in your face. If you start working out, they will try and sabotage your plans. Do you see it takes a lot more inner strength? They are temptations gateway. Oh, you just quit smoking let me blow smoke in your face. Maybe you're on a diet, and they happen to show up with

your favorite dessert because they are so lovely and thought about you. Really, they are just jealous that you are improving your life, but it's spurring them to put the test of self-control, determination, and integrity in front of you. All a necessary component for you to get stronger pushed by their insecurity. Don't be suckered by the charming personality as they offer you that cake. And if you turn it down, don't allow them to shame or use guilt trips to make you feel bad. "Oh, but I spent hours on making you this delicious dessert, it's such a shame that you are on a diet. It would make me so happy if you had a piece." And the voice inside our head that loves the cake and making others happy says what would it hurt to have just one slice. But our higher self knows we have given into temptation, and the inner voice starts rattling away. The narcissist has a divine spiritual purpose in that dynamic and providing us with spiritual tests. Make sure you see them so you keep your emotions in unconditional love, gratitude, forgiveness, and peace with them.

12. Everything you say or do can and will be used against you. Narcissists love to sniff our faults, weakness, anger, shame, guilt, and insecurity. What's happening? The narcissist is voicing any lower emotions we hold against ourselves. They are wired to be messengers of those painful spaces. Use it as a tool to unconditionally love yourself and let whatever feelings come up be recognized and released. You will know you have healed when you no longer have that painful emotional response to those type of attacks. People can only make us feel "bad" in the spaces where we feel "bad" about ourselves. If I joke with you about your weight and you already have self-hate and insecurity about it you will emotionally react. Use the narcissist like you would a blood hound that knows how to sniff and bark at every negative emotion already inside of you so you can heal.

13. You have to make peace with their qualities, so you don't bang your head against the wall. They can't feel guilty, ashamed, or compassionate for other people. Their viewpoint is rationalized,

with them being the victim always and regardless of what you have done. They will twist every situation to make it look like they are the poor, innocent, victim. You are the bad guy, but they are frustrated with themselves, their job, weight, insecurities and faults etc. They are taking it out on you and can't be accountable. I know it can be such a hard hurdle to overstep. We see the narcissist for who they are and realize we have given everything up for them. We handed our power over to someone completely self-centered, sabotaging our happiness, and delighted to see us suffering. You must understand their role in your growth. Otherwise, the resentful, bitter, angry narcissist within will take hold of you. Even if you have decided to leave them and go no contact, the games will continue to roll on as they sabotage you in a new way. Break the chemical loop addiction that entraps you in the negative loop that goes around and around all about them. When you see your thoughts pop up of their offenses, outline every reason it was a match, messenger, and designed to strengthen you. Think of all those weaknesses and imbalances they triggered you to work on by the suffering they created. Once you do the self-work and expand beyond them, you will be grateful for their role in your development and embrace them with unconditional love, forgiveness, and peace.

14. They will have completely false perceptions of situations, the past, people, or experiences that are nowhere in alignment with the truth. Don't argue out their reality of disillusions; it's a waste of time and energy. They live in their fantasy land where they are always the hero, victim, or whatever it is they need to warp to fit their fake reality and get supply. I remember with my first husband. My whole family joked after we split up that I drank the Bill Johnson Kool-Aid. It's true. This necessary component takes over with narcissists. The Kool-Aid makes us blind all for essential reasons. How could we have done all this self-work if we saw them for who they truly are? If you're starting to spot narcissists, be proud of yourself. We are gullible and naïve, before you

would have just fallen down the sucker road. If you're still working on it, start reading articles on spotting liars and manipulators. Watch the tone of their voice. How they present things they are trying to sell you? Anyone who inflates every way they are fantastic or wonderful is an instant way to set off my radar. Most true unhealed empaths will tell you all of their faults, not recognize their strengths, and try to rationalize the negative behaviors of others. Most narcissists will exaggerate themselves while pointing out every flaw in others. Rather than listening to people watch them. Actions are where you will find the truth.

15. While you are working on the messages, healing, and learning to disconnect energetically from the narcissist be patient and loving with yourself. Once you start to see the qualities and interplays happening between you and the narcissist you may hate yourself for staying. In fact, you may have been circling with self-hate about being in the relationship for a long time. This circling of self-hate keeps you in the pattern. When you finally understand all things are being orchestrated on purpose for exact reasons of growth and development you will have inner peace. The judgments of yourself and others is replaced with a sense of complete compassion regardless of the situations you or others find themselves locked into. If you heal and the narcissist stays in their patterns, they will no longer have any use for you. This is the certificate of completion and graduation ceremony. Going "no negative energy" is much more powerful than "no contact" and releases the bonds of attachment that may have led you to feel like a prisoner.

Engaging peacefully with these personality types is entirely possible. It seems like a challenge. As time goes on and you begin healing, it gets easier and easier. You start understanding that they are helping you see those internal cracks and making you stronger. The narcissist is continuously going to try to pull you into their three-ring circus IF you are a good source of SUPPLY. When you can master these relationships, you can be in any situation with anyone and remain stable in yourself. You are no longer the emotional puppet.

They are the professionals at manipulation, games, and illusions. Now they have met their match with the healed version of you stepping up to the plate. Watch how your new set of skills lead you right through their tactics unaffected. You may surprise yourself too. You may leave a marriage with a toxic spouse, or that job you hate, or disconnect from a narcissistic family member. This inner healed version of you will be able to stay in the situation or walk away without feeding the vampire supply. You realize it's entirely up to you. When you pull the energetic plug and deal with them in a healthy balanced way, they may walk out on you. You are no longer a commodity for them.

This may inspire some fear in you that will have to be answered by faith. If your job and monetary life connect to a narcissistic boss, set boundaries, stand your ground, and fight for yourself. A nagging voice in the back of your mind will be throwing you curve balls. What if I get fired or need to walk away to honor myself? How will I support myself? Watch the stories go around in your head. Don't push them away. Do release them and replace them with the positive self-talk. If I get fired, a better situation will fall in my lap.

I trust the Universal Creator/God/Gaia (whoever you believe in) to put a healthy, loving situation on my path. I know everything happens for a reason. I trust that being the authentic healed version of myself, not a slave to my fears, will attract a new reality. The universe is truly amazing at matching our internal issues. You may be surprised the narcissist may step up to the plate. Give you what you are asking for without question. The world was waiting for you to stand up and value you. We must stop being slaves to our anxieties, fears, and negative running programs.

There are no right or wrong answers. Whatever space you find yourself on the path, you can start taking steps to disarm the bomb. Your body and physical experiences have been begging you to pull out that inner God/Goddess. Use these relationships as a road map to become a complete balance.

The good and bad news is you will continue to attract these relationships until you learn everything about YOURSELF, they have been designed to teach you. Your body is much like a light vessel with an electromagnetic field. This is why we get hooked into repeat patterns with toxic people, and even if we see it cannot take steps to get out until the deep level inner work is done. That energetic field is stronger when you learn exactly how to protect it by not allowing others to siphon energy off of you. There's no way to do that without internally getting stronger. The journey is physical, emotional, mental, and energetic or spiritual.

One of my favorite parts of "waking up" has been realizing that the real way my body works is much different than I was taught. Truly most of things I learned in school and through the mass programming was a lie. No one ever mentioned anything about these concepts or the fact my body was running off of energy systems. Only in having experiences with energy and consciousness did I realize that my body and health was very connected to chakra's, meridians, radiant circuits, and internal wiring with codes that I couldn't see.

If narcissists, toxic personalities, and darkness was not here precisely the way it is none of this soul evolution would be possible. There is no such thing as "no contact" when the god/universal force knows you still have lessons that you need to learn from these personality types. Now you know the "destroyers" are the messengers to where the "healing" must happen. They are a creation of divine design and a necessary component of our spiritual, mental, and emotional growth.

This next chapter is meant to introduce those concepts of taking this idea of becoming rock solid to the next level. There are links between our physical, mental, emotional, and spiritual health that require narcissists, Illuminati, manipulative, and controlling psychopaths. When we shift into activating our light body and sealing ourselves off from transferring any energy to the darkness, something amazing happens.

We become the God/Goddess we were initially designed to be regardless of dark situations, circumstances, or people. Our light shines so brightly we are untouchable. The issue with darkness is not about "them" it's about the darkness they trigger within us. The elements of our energetic bodies are crucial components to our mental, emotional, spiritual, and physical health.

"There is no coming to consciousness without pain. People will do anything, no matter how absurd, in order to avoid facing their own soul. One does not become enlightened by imagining figures of light, but by making the darkness conscious." - Carl Jung

CHAPTER 11
SHINING LIGHT

OVER THESE LAST FEW YEARS I've had a whole new awakening. I'm so grateful! Those openings in my reality pushed me to study, understand, and implement an entirely new set of knowledge. Honestly, I was in a very dark place back then, and the depths of it I didn't really acknowledge or fully see until I started building the ladder out. Looking back on it now, I was ultimately so blind and naïve. I couldn't see any of the tactics used against me. What I knew at the core of my soul was I felt dead inside — honestly, just a walking robot.

I always knew there was good and evil. But other than that, nothing here on Earth was what the marketing and advertising told me. I honestly had no clue there was such a thing as an energetic body. Narcissists and Empaths. Reptilians and Pleiadeans. The Illuminati. Everything I thought about the universe, people, and life itself was a lie. Wait?!?! What?!?! Then I uncovered even me, myself, and I was a lie. Not on purpose but trained into belief systems, patterns, attracting my dysfunctional running programs, a slave to my ego, and always working out incoming karma, and unintentionally creating new karma.

I was born with unhealed wounds, spiritual tests I had failed, and lessons I had not learned. All the players, life situations, and being cornered with difficult personalities in my life reflected them.

I had NO CLUE who I was, and if she was buried under there, I was afraid to be her!

And then God blew the cork on me. I started having experiences with energy and consciousness. I began to wonder who am I internally? I was everyone they told me I needed to be. I looked for that praise of being a good mom, wife, friend, a good you name it. What do you need me to be to fit the cookie-cutter mold, so I feel loved? Oh, you need someone to help wipe your ass. What time? I'll be there. You can count on me, hahaha. I was working overtime for everyone as I looked for love and approval. I had attracted a whole slew of "takers." People that wanted to be my friend when it fits their needs and they wanted something.

I was a fake. I was a people pleaser. I was completely miserable in myself and this world.

Oh, look at my social media with my happy family and our perfect life. You would never know. My smile wasn't real. My laugh was not laughter, merely a disguise. I hated my life. I hated my husband. I felt owned by everyone, including my kids, and every day I tried to keep up the facade. Blindly following the protocol for what they say to do to be "happy."

Why am I so unhappy then?

Yes, that was rough to see. Working through myself is truly a non-stop work in progress, but I'm so much clearer and genuinely happier than I've ever been. Being and knowing you're a mess is SOLID GOLD! I don't think I'm alone in this either. So many people are hitting the "dark night of the soul." We are asking more profound questions.

Who am I? Without the people-pleasing. Without caring what society says or advertises. Without the way, I was raised. Who am I letting shape me out of the authentic me? Do I genuinely hate my husband, or is it my inability to deal with him that I hate?

I love my kids! But somewhere, I started blaming them for not pursuing my own goals. I never realized I couldn't set boundaries for myself. I absorbed myself in others to self-avoid.

I hated the way this world works. The governmental control, a jaded economy, Illuminati, suffering, oppression, and every other horrific way we hurt each other ALL THE time. I discovered that I had not spiritually been in my body for years because I would have to face so much here that I didn't want to see. The fact I "checked out" led me to be even more susceptible to gaslighting. If you aren't in your body when someone tells you what happened in the past, you don't know what happened.

I reacted by retreating into the desert and isolating myself. Oh look, I can create my world out here and never have to face the madness out there. I disconnected from the world in lots of ways. We got a milk cow and chickens. I purified my diet. I had my control zone away from society. Yet, I wasn't happy. Beyond the fact that I loved living out, I still wanted to connect with people and life. However, that meant being triggered by my inner trauma and dysfunctional working order reflected in these relationships.

I felt alone, depressed, and disconnected myself.

I am shocked in awakening and healing just how many internal negative emotions I was running all the time. From the outside, you would have never thought I was anything but "happy." Most empaths, I think, are like this. We don't tell everyone about our problems. We don't want to trouble others. Besides, we are too caught up in if everyone is feeling good, happy, and loved. The deep-down issues are not what other people want to hear, and it's definitely not what we want to address. Or even know how to!

I remember sweeping my floor one day and asking God, "Is this it? Is this what I am doing here?" I did not understand how or why a higher power could orchestrate any of this experience. All I saw was suffering around me and it was so intense. I couldn't even watch the news. Then I started to have encounters with energy and consciousness. Talk about a whole new world!

I began to understand I am a spirit turning on and off switches to my electrical body unknowingly. Truly this physical experience in a land of darkness and evil was designed to ignite the God/Goddess inside of me. The following information is not meant to make any health claims. This is my journey and the dots I've connected with having these experiences. Initially, I was horrified. In the long run, this led to an eye-opening awakening to the fantastic way we are designed.

My life was more like a hologram where I was doing spiritual work to become closer to complete balance. Earth was the self-work TV channel, and these people and situations were reflecting elements of myself back to me. If the relationship included some type of suffering, there was a message I needed to unravel. All of this physical, mental, and emotional reality was deeply linked to my energetic body, which no one had ever taught me about!

Yet, when I started to become aware of these new sets of laws and do some research, I found something fascinating. There was a lot of evidence supporting the experiences and awareness that was awakening inside of me. Scientific evidence had identified we live in a holographic universe. I needed to connect the dots and understand this "invisible" world. I realized a new part of my body the spiritual or "energetic" systems created.

I came across the work of people like Ram Dass, Michael Newton, Deepok Chopra, Jung, Osha, David Wilcox and Gregg Braden. I realized there was an energetic field or aura around everything. My daughter started to talk about seeing a set of cords around the physical body. Then I met a healer named Sherry Anshara, who also could see these energetic cords. I started feeling energy. I began to know exactly what it felt like to have a heart chakra shut down. It became blazingly apparent that getting to the heart of this energetic matrix and doing all the personal work to keep those systems open was a key to my health!

A series of questions unfolded like what are these things called chakras? Why do I feel them opening and closing? What is creating these vortexes to flood our bodies with energy when they expand or open and crush organs in their path when they shut down or restrict? I noticed the "energetic ickies" which felt like electrical black ink in my veins. I could see how these energy shutdowns had led to allergies, skin rashes, fibromyalgia, chronic pain, and a host of other diseases. What was going on?

Another healer came into my life, Dolores Cannon. I began to realize that the chakras were not only running these spiritual tests but also contained a running script of all our lifetimes. The body was much more of a vessel deepening ourselves by taking turns being each other. Everywhere I lacked compassion started to unfold for me through this Akashic Record timeline and how these experiences developed, deepened, and strengthened me as a person.

I started connecting dots between the mental, physical, emotional, and spiritual centers. I made new revelations as I could see how that energy related to the physical body as those energetic systems shut down or opened up. They deeply affected the blood flow, oxygen, organs, vital rhythms that happen with the glands, the extensive nervous system, and oh so many things! I deeply understood that keeping these vortices and electrical systems open was crucial for my health.

Puzzle pieces came together as I realized I was operating in "cellular memory" loops or repeat patterns. I had run from ego versus spirit consciousness or had unhealed wounds resurfacing. These repeat patterns were mirrors to where I had not done the soul work to heal completely. Karmic connections started to become very clear in my life. I was aware of how I had made judgments of others or lacked compassion, and then the wheels of destiny had put me in their shoes. As if the body was also a vehicle to experience each other using this game called "life."

I needed the narcissist's as that constant trigger of these storms! Operating in the true self/spirit created rubs between the two forces unseen to the naked eye. In the world of energy and scientifically, it all made sense. Narcissists have no light within themselves. They are naturally a negative charge. Only by tapping into a source can they continue to feed their energetic bodies. Tapping into that source involves you the positive charge. Flipping the switch in you from operating in the true self/spirit or positive emotions to the ego/false-self or negative emotions feeds the dark bodies. But you have to allow that to happen. And in fact, we need these people here on Earth to provide us with these spiritual tests, show us our self-abuse patterns, and strengthen us.

On purpose, dark bodies know all your weak spots to flip those switches in their direction! Not that we are perfect either. We all have our faults, but we feel bad about situations where we accidentally hurt people. The narcissist (dark body) is doing it on purpose. They receive energetic feedback from flipping us into the ego or the negative charge. Empaths (light bodies) hurt other people unintentionally and feel guilty when it happens. They get energetic feedback from helping others and seeing people happy, healthy, and full of love.

These forces are always at work, and either the light bodies allow them to make them stronger, or they fall in the darkness themselves.

THE EMOTIONAL CHARGES

POSITIVE (+)	NEGATIVE (-)
True Self	Ego
Love	Hate
Power	Force
Creative	Competitive
Allowing	Controlling
Accepting	Resisting
Strength	Weakness
Confidence	Doubt
Empowered	Victim
Peace	Stress
Virtue	Guilt
Self-Love	Self-Pity
Acceptance	Judgment
Compassion	Detachment
Harmony	Conflict

Abundance	Lack
Trust	Skepticism
Responsible	Lazy/Irresponsible
Secure	Insecure
Assertive	Aggressive
Faith	Fear
Inspiration	Intimidation

Narcissists are disconnected from being able to have empathy so they can mirror back our dysfunctional parts and create the spiritual tests. Empaths are just not capable of being the person needed to show us these vital elements of our wounded selves. We need the darkness in them to spur this inner trauma and create suffering, so we finally will deal with our issues.

Let's pretend, you're mad at yourself for being lazy. You are in a relationship with an Empath. They will not try to shame, guilt, or make you feel bad about being lazy. An Empath will feel your self-anger and want to make you feel better, even if it means lying to you. As we have discussed narcissists are liars, but we are too. The narcissist, however, is wired to get energy or feedback out of making you feel bad. That way, they can show you where you are angry, ashamed, or reject yourself about XYZ element. Laziness is just an example, but this could be anywhere you have an emotional issue that requires self-work. You will know because you will immediately react to their comments, insults, and attacks.

This is what I have noticed since I started having experiences with feeling energy. There is a connection with the feeling of "ickies" all over while being attacked by the exact qualities, we don't like about ourselves. We are divided from our unconditional self-love and beat ourselves up about being lazy. The narcissist is just voicing the negative inner voice. This shuts down electrical pathways in accordance with the bodies energetic systems.

Have you ever noticed that in relationships usually opposites attract? The lazy person falls in love with the busy body who can't sit down. Each person could use some balancing. Yet, the typical reaction is for them to drive each other crazy and not realize the role they have as a mirror. Physical suffering is the consequence as each person wastes time and energy complaining about the other person, but not working on balancing themselves.

The energetic body has this set of cause-and-effect storms matching up. Everything is related. Having these experiences really opened me up to some key insights. Not just the "ickies" of energy but how it feels in the body to have a chakra or meridian shut down. I really should give you my personal disclaimer on this. These are my experiences and I am sharing them to help others connect dots on what resonates with them. I am not attempting to make any medical claims. Although doing self-work has helped me physically heal, I'm just sharing my personal experience.

Some more examples of this would be when we get into a situation where the narcissist abandon, betrays or abuses us. We stay in the relationship and this energetic wave encompasses the whole body. If you have ever seen shock collars that are used in dog training it's a similar system. If the dog misbehaves you just push the button. The electrical current is sent to reinforce "No". Right action means no electrical consequence.

This is very much what the energetic body feels like to me. God's training system that connects the mental and emotional body being in balance with energetic systems. Narcissists can leave us feeling that way like energetic black ink is running through our veins. There personality characteristics can zap our energy and drain us, if we haven't done the self-work as discussed.

Another key shut down is the heart meridian. When the narcissist is making someone else the high priority while they discard you a very serious energy system collapses connected to our heart. I have noticed for myself an uncontrollable trembling of the left hand, muscles twitches in the left bicep, and a pain in the chest area.

Here is a picture of the heart meridian and how the energy runs. Notice how it connects ending directly to the navel (inner womb), heart (love) and under the left eye (perceptions of the world). We must self-partner and become a solid sense of love, support, and approval to ourselves. If we are attracting this co-dependent, dysfunctional type toxic love it is because we have not done this fully and completely.

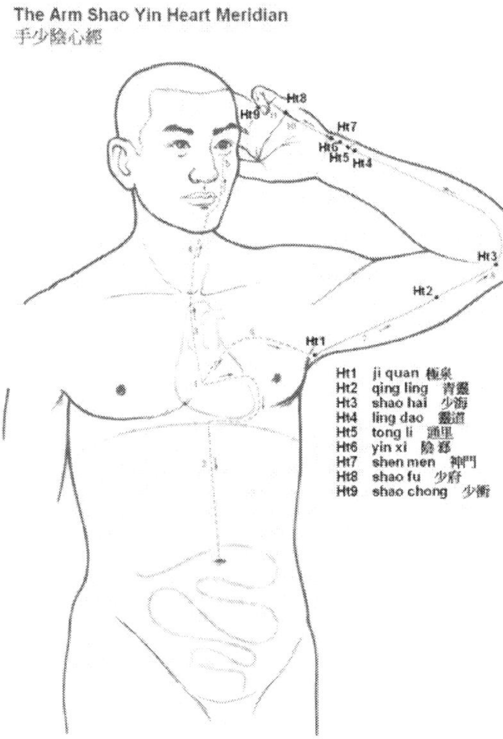

If we are not a solid sense of ourselves or we do not love and adore who we are, how can anyone else? It's the universe's way of trying to communicate with us and address these imbalances. Suffering happens on all levels, physically, mentally, emotionally, and spiritually.

What if a person who does not feel good enough or cannot receive meets another person who can't receive? If anything with money, gifts, or resources is involved, one will jump over the other, trying to give everything away. No here you have it. No you. No you. No one gets to grow or be pushed to balance themselves. If you have not developed a strong identity of who you are, what you think, and are willing to stand up for those principles guess who will be ready to define and use you for your weak sense of self. Narcissists.

If you take anything from this book, I hope it will be the fact we need narcissists, controllers, and the dark forces. There is no judgment, divisions, or lines to separate us. Each counterpart plays a significant role in healing. If there is suffering in a relationship, it is because of an element within that you must address.

Inner wars create outer wars.

Inner peace mirrors back world peace.

Soul pollution mirrors back world pollution.

Violent inner emotional storms mirror back violent physical storms.

Inner balance mirrors back a world that is balanced.

We can profoundly impact the world by working on ourselves. Cherie Carter-Scott's ten rules for being a human really resonate as part of this dynamic...

1. You will receive a body. You may like it or hate it, but it's yours to keep for the entire period.
2. You will learn lessons. You are enrolled in a full-time informal school called, "life."
3. There are no mistakes, only lessons. Growth is a process of trial, error, and experimentation. The "failed" experiments are as much a part of the process as the experiments that ultimately "work".
4. Lessons are repeated until we learn them. A lesson will be presented to you in various forms until you have learned it. When you have learned it, you can go on to the next lesson.
5. Learning lessons does not end. There's no part of life that doesn't contain its lessons. If you're alive, that means there are still lessons to be learned.
6. "There" is no better a place than "here". When your "there" has become "here", you will simply obtain another "there" that will again look better than "here".
7. Other people are merely mirrors of you. You cannot love or hate something about another person unless it reflects to you something you love or hate about yourself.

8. What you make of your life is up to you. You have all the tools and resources you need. What you do with them is up to you. The choice is yours.
9. Your answers lie within you. The answers to life's questions lie within you. All you need to do is look, listen, and trust.
10. You will forget all this.

We are doing much more in this body on Earth than I imagined. Everything in your reality is operating off this invisible energetic system. However, when you break apart your own life, it's easy to see precisely where the trauma, dysfunctional belief systems, imbalances, and fractured pieces of you remain.

Something beautiful happens too as we balance ourselves, heal those inner wounds, and evolve beyond the narcissists. They do not trigger us to feel lower emotions anymore. Let's say you are a doormat. People walk all over you. That's an energetic sticker that attracts people who will walk all over you. What happens when you realize that you are in charge of the energetic labels and start standing up for yourself?

Bossy, controlling, pushy people do not bother you anymore. Not only that, but you see them as a critical insight to exactly how much you have evolved. If someone tries to push you around and you stand up for yourself and the energies of gratitude, unconditional love, and joy open up even further. You recognize exactly how everything in your life has been a beautiful arrangement of everything that is within you. Becoming this perfect orchestration of the "light body" in a land of darkness is the key objective of evolving. Those ready to face themselves will embody "Enlightenment." The greatest spiritualists of all time were looking to achieve this state of being.

I could relate this to all religions, guru's, and other philosophies of thought. The great philosophers like Aristotle have written of the Golden Mean or attaining a balance through this container we call our lives.

ARISTOTLE'S CONCEPT OF THE GOLDEN MEAN

DEFICIENCY (-)	BALANCE	EXCESS (+)
Cowardice	COURAGE	Rashness
Stinginess/ Miserliness	GENEROSITY	Extravagance
Sloth	AMBITION	Greed
Humility	MODESTY	Pride
Moroseness	GOOD HUMOR	Absurdity
Quarrelsomeness	FRIENDSHIP	Flattery
Self-indulgence	TEMPERANCE	Insensibility
Apathy	COMPOSURE	Irritability
Indecisiveness	SELF CONTROL	Impulsiveness

Lots of times in soul mate relationships, opposites will attract as teachers to one another. The hard, critical, strict disciplinarian attracts the overly relaxed, easygoing, constant giver. The tightwad attracts the excessively generous. The loud and obnoxious attracts the quiet and meek. The overly negative finds the overly positive outlook. Balancing ourselves is no easy task. Until we do, these opposites continue to attract and drive each other crazy. In my opinion your body works similar to a magnet.

One deficiency or excess is not better than the other. They are facets of ourselves where we need to grow and evolve. If you get lost in the judgments or being a victim of the situation, you will miss the whole point. The key reason that you have attracted this person is lost, and the magnetic charges will keep you locked into them. Beyond that, the energetic body will open and close according to your behavior and reactions to situations.

Eastern religions talk about this electrical body of charges extensively. The chakras, meridians, and many elements of our electrical or spiritual body are commonly discussed. I wasn't ever exposed to these energetic systems. It was only in feeling them opening and closing that I started to study them extensively. Why? Why wasn't I educated that the foundation of ALL things is energy, frequency, and vibration? Here is the foundation of all life, and it seemed to me they had kept it a secret.

The most significant energetic system I feel intensely are the chakras and the electrical grid. The chakras work much like a vortex pulling energy into the body when being open. When they are closed, they run like a tornado over the Earth, except they affect your physical body. That means if your heart chakra is closed, the energy is spinning a centrifugal force pushing on the physical body. It's like putting a 50-pound weight on your heart, thymus, and lungs and then asking them to pump correctly. In my personal opinion and based on my energetic experiences these chakras all affect the physical body profoundly.

The heart chakra shutdowns are the most intense to feel. Gregg Braden and the iheartmathinstitute on YouTube has some great videos posted on this amazing electromagnetic field. I highly recommend watching them if you have internet access or reading some of his books. Hearing these same concepts in different ways from different healers will help you to understand and apply what I am saying in these pages.

Our bodies are intricately designed in deep connection with our outside "Earth." Chakras are energetic tornadoes all over your body. As we swirl with emotional storms these energetic storms open and close. The damage that will be done is in accordance with the level of the emotional storm.

Have you ever seen what a hurricane or a tornado can do to a town? Buildings rip apart. If you consider these chakras are located over physical organs and glands, then you understand the implications. This in my opinion and experience with energy is why modern medicine is failing us completely. How is a heart specialist with no knowledge of how the heart chakra works going to understand something like an arrhythmia, heart attack, or other issues?

In case you don't know, a heart arrhythmia is an irregular heartbeat that occurs when the electrical impulses do not work correctly. Something I struggled with before my understanding and awakening of the energy body. Think about it. What is a pacemaker or defibrillator? It's an electrical device that keeps heartbeats in their correct rhythm. If needed, it will send an electrical shock to the heart.

We need to look at what is happening emotionally. When the pacemaker gets triggered, something emotional is going on in life. The heart chakra shut down is the reason for the hearts malfunction. How is your heart supposed to pump if it's crushed by that invisible energy field creating the tornado? It literally feels like someone is just stepping right on my heart, with a pulling on my shoulders. How can the heart pump the way it needs to in order to maintain health? These are vital keys we need to really be open to looking at and inspecting.

If you study these chakras, they run all along the body. Let's look at the throat chakra. What happens when you don't say what you feel? In my body it's just like getting choked with the center of the pressure on your thyroid. How can the thyroid regulate your body when it's squished between your hands? All the major chakras are in the pathways of the glands. Everything is deeply interrelated to the energy body when it comes to our health. Sherry Anshara has a great book, "The Age of Inheritance," that helps explain these concepts. Look for mine coming soon!

Often, if we can hear theories in different ways from many people, things will click for us. Honestly, without the experiences of feeling them being open and closed, I would never have taken them so seriously. My posture and body alignment have even changed in doing self-work and energy healing. I had no idea this invisible world was destroying my organs and wrecking my health. I was completely clueless about energy systems period. I want to be very clear I am not making any health claims just sharing my experiences with energy.

There is a chiropractor that I came across during my hunt to understand these experiences linking emotions to energy systems. His name is Dr. Bradley Nelson and he has a huge amount of work out right now. In his journey he discovered that emotions created misalignments. This completely makes sense if you think about the energy systems pushing and pulling like tornados on the spine. I started to notice these connections in my journey studying other healers.

Some common examples would be hump back shoulders with the chest caving in as a reflection of heart chakra shutdowns (weak boundaries and self-love). If the neck seems to jut forward along with the head or someone has thyroid issues, that's a throat chakra indicator. (difficulty expressing truth) If you could see the glands they are also directly located at the center of these vortexes. When you are not running in the positive archetype, you put those body parts in a vice grip. They can't work effectively. There is energy spinning and weaving around you all the time. This constant ebb and flow opens and closes as we go through life and handle people, situations, and relationships.

Most people familiar with Eastern medicine will recognize and be familiar with these systems. However, I was raised with zero knowledge of my energetic body. Everything I discovered was foreign to me. Yet it was the keys to health. Illness starts with the energy systems. Wow, that was seriously a big headline idea for me. Now I could attest to its power. I felt the repercussions of these openings and the closing of myself and others.

The chakra's open and close on a system of switches that run off being emotionally balanced (open) or unbalanced (closed). In terms of being in relationships with narcissists a lot of energetic shutdowns can happen in situations revolving around them. Here are some of the biggest examples.

CROWN:	No longer connected to God or the universal creator. Or overly connected to floating, daydreaming, and other forms of "not being present" and in your body. Seeking an escape from your physical reality.
BROW:	The ego desires control to fix, heal, and save everyone without knowing how to let go and trust everything is working in its perfect order. I know we have opposite reasons, but we still seek to control in order to heal, fix, and have harmony thinking it is found outside of us rather than within.
THROAT:	When you do not speak up for yourself, your truth, or express your feelings.

HEART:	When you let someone walk all over you and become a doormat for others. Can't set boundaries.
SOLAR PLEXUS:	If you feel powerless and out of control of your own life.
SACRAL:	If you do not become the "mother" and "father" of your own nurturing, care, and love. Co-dependent to a dysfunction. Looking for a parent outside of themselves rather than within.
ROOT:	When you hand your power of survival to another person rather than trusting in yourself and the universe. Whoever you assign that power to must fail you, as you have failed yourself.

Realize this is extremely simple and the energetic body is worth a whole book itself. In fact, there are many written on it. I'm just introducing the concepts and will publish more on this as time goes on. I have a YouTube video that further explains this concept. You can access it by clicking this link. https://www.youtube.com/watch?v=F0gG7KGEGnI There are many other healers talking about our energy bodies. I will put a list of recommended reading at the end of the book.

In my experiences and so many others there is an invisible field running the show here. It's fascinating and a crucial missing link in modern education!

The meridians are the second-largest energetic system, although the bodies energetic field is more complicated than these two systems, I want to keep it simple. If you interested in exploring more about the meridians you can find my YouTube explanation by clicking this link https://www.youtube.com/watch?v=oO2-XAfBXtw. I believe this energy body is the true "spirit". In order to be operating in harmony you need to balance yourself. The emotional balances or imbalances create electrical charges. The energy is either shocking you (I mean this), shut down, or open and flowing. Think about this like rivers. If the water is blocked or jammed up, then what happens to all the life the river feeds with its precious water.

Or in situations where it's sending an electrical shock wave, what effects does that have?

Sounds easy when you look at it all organized in cute little charts. However, add in our dysfunctional systems, fears, anxieties, inner trauma, and things get messy. If you visit an acupuncturist or energy healer, they will access these systems and rebalance the energies. However, all voltages are always ebbing and flowing according to drumroll please... life situations, people, and these inner traumas. Meaning you could walk out the door of the acupuncturist, get home to your spouse who starts ranting and raving, and find that the energy shuts down again.

When these pathways hit emotional meltdowns, the flow of energy cannot feed the body and the organ it is associated with to function properly. Meaning the physical body is interlaced with the energetic body that connects deeply to our emotions, mind, and spiritual tests like the tides in the ocean ebbing and flowing with the rhythm of the universe. Their harmony working with your body is in direct correlation to your emotional, mental, and spiritual balance.

The Chinese Medicine Wheel interlaces these meridians together with each component reflecting an emotion, body part, season, and element of the physical world. We do not educate ourselves and our children on how these systems all work in unison together. As a homeschooling parent, I am working on a whole body of work called "Conscious Curriculum." It will be a great program to assist people in educating their children. When there is a blockage of an emotion like anger, it throws the balance of the whole wheel off.

Something I want to expand on a little more is an electrical grid that runs over our bodies. Could this have a linking to mystery illnesses like fibromyalgia, chronic pain, inflammation, unexplainable fatigue, body rashes, food allergies, and lowered immune system? This energetic system shuts down and gives the feeling of the "ickies" all over. It's like black ink running through your veins except its electrical.

When we are in relationships with a narcissist, they trigger us into seeing elements of ourselves that we dislike. The universe corners us with these people who are firing the gun at us by their constant criticisms, boundary-pushing, and tactics. They know every element we reject about ourselves, and that's precisely when the "ickies" all over hit. Another person reflects an internal unresolved soul issue.

For example, let's say you have weak boundaries. The narcissist has just been rude, demeaning, and it's clear they are openly using you. However, you stay with them because of some internal fear. You recognize you are being mistreated by them but remain in the relationship. Or they've just pulled a complete jerk move and then say, "Come give me a kiss." You, being full of these unresolved traumas and people-pleasing issues, do go over and kiss them even though you don't want to at a soul level. That's when the "ickies" all hit and the electrical feeling of black ink going through your WHOLE-BODY hits!

Another example is every time someone triggers something you hate about yourself. Our ego's can be such tricky beasts. Sometimes we just give up and stay with the narcissist because the ego tries to convince us this is the "easy way". Our inner voice and highest selves know the truth and nag in the back of our minds at us. If we are just staying in a comfort zone to avoid facing fears, or living our full potential our lives trap us with people that show where we have given up. Relationships we don't enjoy. Jobs we don't like. Living arrangements.

These energetic/spiritual connections link everything together through a matrix that attracts us to these relationships and all life situations with the world. This is the basis of diseases that mystify the current medical community (once again my opinion). A beautiful system of energy that ebbs and flows in rhythms over the body. Have you ever seen the health nut that was very healthy, exercised daily, and took great physical care of himself but died suddenly of a heart attack at age 52? No one can understand it in the medical community.

He was so careful about doing the right things. Yet at an energetic level, he most likely had a profound amount of heart chakra shutdowns. Wouldn't a doctor feel the call to fix, heal, and save everyone? Every day he sees patients and their families looking to him for answers, yet he is on mission impossible! People die and suffer from diseases they don't understand daily. Facing situations like this constantly has his electrical body shutting down his heart chakra consistently. The healers of this Earth must learn these concepts. Otherwise, they will just completely frazzle out. Burnout! Even the words hit home as a reflection of the emotional and energetic field.

Narcissists are entirely disconnected and self-absorbed, but Empaths are overly connected to everyone and everything. If Empaths do not learn that they cannot fix, heal, and save everyone, these heart chakra shutdowns take over. Doctors want to be the magic man. At this point in our evolution using current methodologies, he's only looking at the body on a physical level. Facing every day where he needs to learn where to let go. Know he is doing his best to help every patient, but he is not God/Creator. Balancing the internal scales would open the heart and brow chakras.

All of us may have different issues but the bottom line is the same. Energy flows opening and closing according to our actions, emotions, and place of evolution. The universe's working order of all things happening perfectly is impressive. Even the worst of situations carry growth and meaning. The energetic body also brings a lot of coded information. All of this is important in attracting back to us the exact circumstances we need to heal our emotional issues completely. Much of what we have talked about already.

Imbalances (Opposites Attract)

Mirrors (Other people are like looking into a soul mirror.)

Ego Entrapments (The ego is a beastly ruler if left unattended running your show.)

Belief Systems (Money is the root of all evil.)

Past lifetimes unresolved traumas (if you believe in reincarnation) or generational karmic loads (if you believe in genetics).

Spiritual tests that have not been jumped. (The narcissist just got the job promotion you wanted even though you are more skilled, hardworking, and reliable. Will you drop into anger, bitterness, jealousy, or the many ego emotions that could get triggered?)

Everywhere we lack compassion is attracted back to us to soften us towards each other. Karma.

This energetic coding spurs the laws of attraction in bringing all the players and situations into our lives to work out these places. Our lives are a moving picture show continuously outputting this energetic blueprint. These different players in our lives are mirroring back to us everything we need to know about the inner world. The keys to healing are in your own hands, but you have to take action.

The knowledge is so empowering! We all have control of doing the soul work to operate at our highest potential and divine state of consciousness. No one will come to save us. That's how these energetic bonds attract us to one another. If the charges still line up, it doesn't matter how many people, jobs, or relationship dynamics you walk away from. New people, situations, and relationship dynamics show up mirroring the same old internal issues. These are called the laws of attraction.

You are in charge of YOU!

This messy, dark, complicated world is by design to push you to the very edges of yourself.

That's why every part of your body is related and interconnected with emotions, unhealed or healed wounds, running programs functional or dysfunctional, and spiritual tests jumped or failed. We receive messages every single day, pinpointing where we need to do soul work. A thought, memory, or emotion gets triggered by some relationship, situation, or life experience. If this is an adverse reaction, there is a disruption or blockage in the energy's flow system. Then there is the suffering that ensues from the physical, emotional, or psychological pain.

Every present moment is your teacher. Every space you fall into negative emotions is communicating with you. Nothing here is happening without it being necessary. If it weren't these players in life, it would be someone else playing out this role for growth. Different messengers are carrying the same repetitive patterns. Have you ever seen someone go through a divorce, and then they hook up with a new partner who's just like the one they left?

Repeat patterns continue to persist until we go on this epic journey. No one can do it for you, and these cycles of toxic personalities are not going anywhere until you face yourself. For as long as I can remember I wanted to change the world. End suffering. Stop so many criminal systems that prevail. Now I understand that all of these elements are exactly as they need to be to reflect our inner dysfunctions and present us a training ground to grow and heal. The world is exactly as it needs to be to change us.

This is the "time" to heal our wounds, balance ourselves, run the new programming, and continuously keep our energetic/spiritual systems OPEN all the time regardless of the situation. We need to decode the jungle and learn what switches are running what lights. If there is suffering, something has yet to be learned, evolved, or developed within us. For those ready to take this journey true enlightenment will occur!

Until then you know where you are...

You're in the jungle, baby.

Final Notes and Thoughts

I have many other publications coming soon, including a narcissists journal. This will be a great addition to this book. It will show you how life experiences mirror internal soul dilemma's and the personal work that needs to be done in order to heal, up-level, and evolve. If you like my work and would like to be informed on new publications, coupon codes, FREE DAYS, and special discounts sign up to be on my email list. You can find me online at https://www.narcissistnirvana.com and on YouTube. Check out my channel Truth Bomber TV:

https://www.youtube.com/channel/UCUmMXxIgUPvmYT0mlLs3ilA?

There are also a lot of other authors that have reinforced my experiences with energy and consciousness plus published works to help expand our ideas of what we really are doing here. The physical body and our spirits are so much more than we are led to believe.

If you are interested in learning more, here are a few other people that you maybe interested in checking out.

Michael Newton

Donna Eden

Dolores Cannon

Gregg Braden

David Wilcock

Sherry Anshara

Christie Marie-Sheldon

Dr. Bradley Nelson

David Wilcock

Carl Jung

We are in a fascinating period of evolution. For those people who are ready and willing to start doing inner work reality will change completely. The ending of the "dark ages" or suffering will end. People will live much longer lifetimes as the emotional and spiritual healing has physical affects. Not only that but they will enjoy life and be using the body and the spiritual gifts they carry to become the highest versions of themselves.

This is the era of the "Enlightenment"!

Made in the USA
Columbia, SC
22 February 2021

33399988R00117